THINK
and be
UNSTOPPABLE

JOSH RACIOPPO

ISBN: 978-1-922409-08-9
Published by Vivid Publishing
A division of Fontaine Publishing Group
P.O. Box 948, Fremantle
Western Australia 6959
www.vividpublishing.com.au

A catalogue record for this
book is available from the
NATIONAL
LIBRARY   National Library of Australia
OF AUSTRALIA

This book is dedicated to Viktor Frankl, whose courageous use of his mind enabled him to survive the concentration camp at Auschwitz.

INTRODUCTION

"It's me against the world." Have you ever heard that saying? Many people go through their lives believing that the big bad universe is out to get them. Nothing ever seems to go right for them. They jump from problem to problem without hope of ever escaping the rat race and finally becoming successful.

Is that you right now? Does one of your years run into the next year with no change? Would you like things in your life to change?

If things have been this way for you, that's OK, because throughout this book I will help you see ways in which you can turn your whole life around.

In my previous book, *If You Change, Everything Will Change*, I highlighted the need to make the changes to ourselves that will put us on track to achieving great success and living the life we have always wanted.

How would you like to become unstoppable? Unstoppable seems to be a word that we don't often use about ourselves.

When I hear the word unstoppable, I think of a train.

If a train is going at full speed, what person, what object, could stop this beast? Who could possibly bring it to a halt? I am sure you would agree with me that there are not a lot of things that can stop a freight train going at full speed.

That's the thought I will try and convey to you in this book. The thought that you can be like a freight train and become unstoppable in your life.

That no matter what emerges in front of you, whatever comes into your life, be it people or events, you will not be stopped.

It could be financial problems, family issues, work-related dilemmas or it could be something internal. If the world is crumbling around you, it won't have an effect on you if you are unstoppable. No matter what is in front of you, you will be able to plough right through it and keep on going. You will have a strong conviction and a firm grip on your values and your life goals and, most importantly, your happiness.

From the moment you finish this book and start applying its principles, you will never let anybody look down on you or belittle you again.

You will wake up every morning loving your life and loving where you are heading.

Everybody wants to be successful in their lives, but unfortunately very few end up truly succeeding.

If success was a thing handed to you at birth, things would be different, but unfortunately it is not granted to everyone. Everyone can be successful, but only the ones who truly become unstoppable will be successful in all areas of their lives.

If you want to be successful, you will need to make changes in your life so that success will come to you. You will attract the life you want by becoming an attractive person.

After you finish this book, you will never again say that the universe is against you. You will come to realise that the universe is there to help you have an amazing life and the reason that's not happening for everyone is because most people see the universe as an enemy instead of a friend.

The universe is like a genie saying to you, "Your wish is my command." Why not do what successful people do and partner with the universe to become unstoppable?

Life will pay whatever price you ask of it.

I have found this to be true in my life and it can be true for you too.

I love every aspect of my life. I live a carefree, happy, successful life.

I say this to you not to impress you, but to impress upon you that if I can live this way, you can too. You see, as I often tell people, I didn't finish high school. The truth is, I really stopped listening to schoolteachers when I was in grade eight. I am not saying that kids should drop out of school, I am just saying that it was my self-education after I left school that helped me create the life I have now.

I am not saying that there are never any problems in

life, but I will show you how to deal with them when they come up.

Like I mentioned in the introduction of my last book, I am not a writer, I am an entrepreneur and world traveller, but I wanted to try and put into writing the things that have made my life a success.

Similarly to my last book, I have applied a conversational style to my writings, so it's as if you and I are sitting down having a chat. You don't have to believe everything I say. If you don't agree with something, then just discard it. If you agree with it, then please put it into practice in your life.

I do ask you one thing. If things in your life are not going the way you want, then please take everything I say on board as truthful, because I don't lie.

Let me use an example to explain the attitude I had when I started learning the things that would help me improve my life many years ago.

Once upon a time, there was a poor man walking down the street looking in one rubbish bin after another and taking out scraps of food. A rich man saw this as he was driving down the road.

The rich man decided to pull his car over and talk to the poor man. After pulling his Rolls-Royce to the side of the road, he hopped out with his creaseless suit shining brightly and his Rolex watch sparkling on his wrist.

The rich man called the poor man over to him and asked him if he could speak to him and give him some financial advice so he wouldn't have to search the bins for food anymore. The poor man waddled over and the rich man spent ten minutes telling him how he could make money and start living a better life. After the rich man was finished, the poor man gazed at him thinking about what he had just said. After a few seconds, the poor man said to the rich man, "No, I don't think your advice will work." He then turned around and headed for the nearest rubbish bin. The rich man was amazed and per-plexed. He had offered this poor man specific ways of making money that could change his life forever and he was rejected for a rubbish bin.

I tell this story because when I first started making changes in my life, I was nothing like that poor man. I read many books and listened to lots of audio programs and I believed everything I heard. I realised that the men on the tapes and the authors of the books I read, are in a much better position than I was, so I believed them, and I am glad that I did.

Success means different things to different people. The best definition of success I have heard is that success is the ongoing realisation of a worthy ideal. Whether you want to make a million dollars or sell up and go and live on a farm and feed the animals, you are a success.

Whatever your goals are, as long as you are heading in the direction of achieving them you are a success. As you go through this book, there will be a lot of things that you can apply in your life straightaway to start seeing results very quickly.

I care about you and I want you to succeed, because if

I meet you one day, I want to see an unstoppable person who is loving life. Be that person, be like Joe.

Once upon a time there was a man named Joe. One day, Joe steadily walked up to the base of a massive mountain. He looked up to the top of the mountain and with all the strength he could muster, he yelled out with a loud voice, "I am climbing you all the way to the top. Either I reach the top or I will die trying. You will either see me at the top waving my flag or rolling down the side dead. Either way, here I come."

At that moment, the ground gently rumbled. All of a sudden, the mountain decided to call a quick meeting. The mountain gathered Wind, Gravity, and Time together and said to them, "Did you hear what Joe just said? He said that he is going to climb this mountain to the top or he will die trying and I think he is serious. We had better give him what he wants."

I want you to be like Joe. I want you to become unstoppable or die trying. When you are that determined, somehow the universe will step aside and let you have all that you want.

Today is your first day on this beautiful planet. You never will be the same again.

For all new arrivals, I hand them a *Welcome to Earth* pamphlet. Here is yours.

Welcome to this beautiful planet, this jewel of our galaxy. You have come here to enjoy your life to the full. There are two ways you can live on this planet, option A or option B. Only you can choose which option you will take. Unfortunately, the majority of people pick option B. I implore you not to choose this option.

Life in option B is like this. You will wake up every morning not excited about your day. You will leave your house and go and work at a job that you hate. You will walk down the street not seeing any of the beauty of Creation.

When something goes wrong in your life, you will blame everyone else. You will blame the most unlikely things because you don't want to admit that it's your fault. You will live one day after another and not go anywhere or learn anything. You will learn a lot in the first year, but then you will repeat that year over and over again for the rest of your life. You will live a life full of drama and problems.

You won't look after your health, so you will age quickly and one day you will not be well enough to work, so you will put your hand out and ask the Government to give you money so you can live the last ten to twenty years of your life without working, if you are lucky.

You will end up dying broke, unhealthy, and unhappy, not having achieved any of your goals.

Can you see why I say don't take option B?

Here is what is in store for you if you choose option A.

Welcome to Earth
From this day forward, you will start learning but never think you have learnt it all, thus always expanding your mind. You will wake up every day with a smile on your

face because you love this gift of life accompanied by a beautiful planet to live on which provides for all your needs.

You will do a job that you love, and if you start not enjoying what you do, you will search for something you love. Since you love yourself, you will love other people and they will treat you well. They will treat you well because of the person you are becoming. You won't let anything negative come into your life because you will constantly monitor your thoughts. The soldier who guards your mind will only allow happy, positive things to come into your mind and you can go about your life with a spring in your step.

When a problem arises, you will take full responsibility for it and so you will either be able to fix the problem or, if you cannot do that, you can do something about your attitude towards the problem. You will never again let people look down on you without your permission to do so.

You will look after your health by doing the things that bring good health. You will believe that you can have anything you want, you will set some good goals and believe you can achieve them because you know that there is a Creator who created this magnificent planet and that because He created you in His image, you have amazing creative powers.

Each day will be a joy, because you will be constantly grateful for life and you will take time to enjoy Creation and just marvel at it.

As the years go on, you won't need to work anymore, because you will have created a life that doesn't need any money from the Government, where you can work for joy and do what you want, when you want, and how you want. Life will be blissful.

Please, choose option A. Start your first day on Earth with the right attitude and with purpose and then life will pay whatever price you ask.

ONE

I was raised in a small town of six thousand people in Victoria, Australia. The town was named after Winston Churchill, something that I didn't understand until I grew up. It was a great town to grow up in for a kid. It was a safe place to grow up and we rode our bikes and played in the parks with no fear of danger.

My parents migrated to Australia from Italy in the middle of last century. They came from a country that had just finished a great war after a great depression. The mentality they learnt about making a living was to get a job and work hard and raise a family.

Starting your own business or investing was not spoken about much in our household when I was growing up. The thought was that you should get a job working for a good company. My father worked at the power station and my mother did casual work at a few different companies.

All in all, it was a good childhood. It wasn't until I grew up that I realised how that idea of finding a good job and working for someone was not the way to go. It wasn't my parents' fault; they were raised with this mentality. Their parents went through the great depression and the war years. These were times where you had to work very hard and save all your money because you didn't know when you might need it in an emergency.

That was my thinking growing up. When I was nineteen, I moved to the big city – Melbourne, Australia. I came to the city carrying my parents' thoughts on making money. I found a full-time job and at the end of the week my pay cheque was a grand total of $500 after tax was taken out. I kept working and finding different jobs and even did some labouring work for a while, but as I got older nothing was changing for me. In my mind, as I got older things were supposed to get better, but nothing was getting better and I never got ahead with my finances.

After some time of things not changing, I started to play the blame game. I blamed the government, because when I looked at my pay cheque I realised how much money they took in taxes. At that time I was upset to have to pay taxes. I also blamed living expenses. Everything cost too much and I wondered why it cost more to live in the city than in the country. I blamed other people for not giving me better opportunities. I blamed my boss because I worked so hard and I was not getting paid what I thought I deserved. I blamed everyone and everything.

There was one person I did not blame, one person who I thought had nothing to do with how my life was going, one person who knew it all and could never be wrong. That person was me.

I had an ego the size of the moon and I could never be wrong, so I could never be the reason why I was not getting ahead in my life. More time went by and one fateful night when I was riding my motorbike I was hit by a big car at high speed. It was my fault. I flew unconscious into the air and woke up in the middle of the road with a kind man helping me up.

Little did I realise that in one swift moment my life would change forever. After spending one month in hospital, I came out with a fractured vertebra, a broken arm, two punctured lungs, and ten severely fractured ribs.

I left the hospital thinking things would have to change. I made a speedy recovery and I was completely back at work in two months.

This time there was no one to blame except myself, but for some reason it still didn't click in my head that I was the reason my life had turned out the way it did.

One day not long after my accident, I heard one sentence that changed my life. In all of my life, this sentence is one of two that have had a major impact on my life.

It's from a man named Jim Rohn, an entrepreneur and public speaker, who said, "If you will change, then everything will change for you." He went on to say that if you don't change, the next five years of your life will be the same as the last five years.

For some reason this sentence had more of an impact on my life than getting hit by a car and nearly dying ever did.

I hope this sentence has as much impact on you as it did on me. If you can instil the essence of this statement into your mind and really think about it, it will change your life. This sentence cuts through everything and puts all the blame on you.

This sentence may hurt you a little because it is not easy to admit to yourself that you are the reason why your life is not where you would like it to be. My ego was cut down from the size of the moon to the size of a little stone.

So, I make a promise to you here and now on this day, that if you will change, your whole life will change. If you change how you think, how you feel, your attitude, your beliefs, your thinking, your habits, your actions, and your goals, if you change everything, then everything will change for you.

Doing the same thing over and over again and expecting a different result is absolute madness.

It's like if you keep planting seeds to grow carrots but expect to grow potatoes. You can keep repeating this process over and over again, but you will never get potatoes from planting carrot seeds.

You cannot keep doing the same things in your life, living the same way, and expect things in your life to change. If you want your life to change, you have to change things in your life. If you make massive changes in your life, you will get massive results. If you just change a few things, then you will only get a few results.

My goal for you is to become unstoppable and to make all of your goals come true and for you to live a happy, successful, and carefree life.

You may say that it's impossible to live that sort of life. I am here to tell you that's not true. I live that life and many people I know or read about live that life, but they only reached that point by changing everything that was not working for them in their life.

Can you see why the phrase, "If you will change, everything will change," had such a great impact on my life?

If I was just waiting for things in my life to change, I was relying on other people to come and save me. My question to you is, what if they don't come? Will you be happy living an average life for the rest of your life?

I am a spiritual person and I believe in a Creator. If you also believe in a Creator, then you realise how powerful humans are. If we were made in our Creators' image and He is the grand Creator, then wouldn't it be reasonable to think that He made us with creative abilities?

You are a creator; you just have to start creating your life and to stop waiting for the rescue boat that may never come. You can be an unstoppable person, it's up to you.

I like the fact that I have the power to change things. It excites me because I can start straightaway. I can start eating an apple a day for my health. Jim Rohn used to say that an apple a day keeps the doctor away. What if that were true? It would be easy to do, but it's also easy not to do it. If you just start with something so simple, like an apple a day for your health, this leads to the next step which will lead to the next step until you are in optimal health.

If you do this with your relationships and your finances and internally with your confidence and self-esteem, can you see how exciting your life will be?

Start with something small and you will see great changes. The first step is realising that you are the reason why your life is the way it is, and it is not the fault of anyone else.

Life change does not need to be a massive undertaking, it's just doing little things every day.

It's not about doing extraordinary things, it's about doing ordinary things extraordinarily well.

Practising the fundamentals on a daily basis.

As the saying goes, "I am not afraid of the thousand kicks you have practised once; I am afraid of the one kick you have practised a thousand times."

As examples, what would be of greater value, eating one apple a day or eating seven apples on Sunday? What is of greater value, running a half an hour every day for your health or running for three and a half hours on Sunday?

It's doing the little things every day that makes the difference.

We will talk more later about the changes you can make, changes in your confidence, self-esteem, goal setting, and much more.

But the first step is realising that you have the power inside of you to make all the changes that you need to make.

I am not sure where in your life I find you right now. Maybe you are displeased about what is going on in your life. If that is the case, then great. From this moment on you don't ever have to be the same, you don't need to keep doing the same things. It starts with an apple a day, a run around the block, and reading books.

Learning from people who are already where you want to be is very important if you want to change. Why reinvent the wheel? Why try to figure it out on your own? Why not imitate, mirror, follow someone who has already done it.

If someone has written a book about how he has changed his life over the years, why would you not read it? You can learn in a few hours what someone has learnt over many years.

If I have found you at a time where you are loving your life, then that's great, that's fantastic. By continuing to read this book, you can refine how you think and how you act. In this book I will give you specific things to do and philosophies that you can think about.

One thing is really important, this I cannot stress enough, the biggest change that you can make is in your mind. This is the start of all change. If you don't change how you think, then you'll keep getting the same results.

When I started changing my mind, I had to remember that my thinking was what got me to where I was and if I wanted to go further my current thinking would not take me there.

I realised that my mind needed a tune-up and that is where I started.

Finances are an example. I have read many books about making money. In every book, they almost all say the same things, It's all about your thinking. They don't tell you how to make money, because there are too many ways and you won't be able to improve your finances until you change your thinking.

I will talk more about this person later, but towards the beginning of last century a man named Napoleon Hill wrote a book, *Think and Grow Rich*. It is interesting that he didn't name his book, 'Buy Properties and Grow Rich' or 'Invest in Shares and Grow Rich.' No, he called it *Think and Grow Rich*. Whether it's making money, improving your health, improving your relationships, becoming more confident, or becoming unstoppable, it all starts in the mind, with our thinking.

I am going to emphasise this again, but do you see how important that phrase is – "If you will change, everything will change"? If you change your thinking, you will be amazed how your life will change. We will talk about thinking and feelings later, but first I want to emphasise this now. There will be many times when I repeat myself in this book. If I do, it is because I really want the point that I am making to affect you like it affected me.

As I mentioned earlier, one of the hardest things that I had to deal with was my ego.

I grew up with a big ego, but it wasn't until I started changing the way I thought that I gained a balance within my personality. I became a very confident person, but not an arrogant person.

So, when I started making changes I had to get rid of my ego and come to the realisation that I had done some things the wrong way. If you feel this way too, then you will have to come to a similar realisation. You have to banish your ego. You don't need it anymore. Being egotistical is a massive hindrance in life.

Confidence is an excellent quality to have, but not arrogance. It is your own abilities and beliefs that make you a confident person. Arrogance is when you think that because of your abilities you are better than others. Please never think this way, especially when success flows your way.

The only way that you will change your life is by changing your mindset, changing your thinking. You will need to become teachable. Unfortunately, when many people grow up they feel they know all they need to know. These people are not teachable.

In the 1950s, two men who pioneered personal development via audio tapes made many recordings and sold them to many people. They thought that they should target the ones who really needed the information, but they were wrong. They realised the ones who bought their tapes were the people who were already successful, who were refining their skills, not the ones who were unsuccessful.

I have found the same thing in my life. The saying goes that leaders are readers and I have found this to be true. They are the ones who want to continue to learn and they are the most teachable.

Teachability is such an important step in changing your life. If you were not feeling well and you went to the doctor to get better, would you listen to his advice or would you walk out and say he doesn't know what he is talking about? If you walked out of his office in disbelief of what he said, it could affect your health badly. It is the same with our life in general. If you are not teachable, will you ever get better?

Something I often wondered about in the past was that if the only way to change your life was to be teachable and not let ego get in the way, then why do I see so many successful people on TV who seem arrogant and seem not to listen to anyone?

Many of these people who started from not having much in life were not that way in the beginning. When they first started, they were very teachable and they didn't have a big ego but unfortunately if we don't change other aspects in our life, then great success can also bring these negative qualities. If we are not careful, this could happen to us.

You may be thinking now, "OK, I am realising I need to change things in my life, but how can I start?"

Start somewhere small and this will lead to other things that you can do. Start with the seven-day challenge. It won't be easy at the start, but if you stick with it the changes to your life will be remarkable. I know people who started the challenge but gave up when they failed a few times. I exhort you to stick with it! Here is the challenge.

For the next seven days, whenever you realise you have a negative thought in your mind, within three seconds I want you to change your thinking to positive. How you do this is up to you. Personally, I say the word "erase" aloud and switch to something positive. Depending on the thought, I generally can just push it out of my mind with the word "erase". If it is a big negative thought, you may need to replace it with a positive thought that will force it out of your head.

Here is the big challenge. You have to do this for seven days straight. If you find yourself thinking negatively before the seven days are up, you need to start the seven days again. You most likely will fail in the first hour and then in the first few days. Therefore, you will have to start the seven days again, but that's OK. You are training your brain to reject anything negative.

You can help yourself by not watching or listening to negative things. I would recommend that you don't listen to, watch, or read the news. It is full of negative things that will put your mind in a negative state.

People say to me that they have to know what is going on in the world but I know many highly successful people who completely disagree with them. Knowing about all the murders, suicides, violence, and terrorism will never help you, but it will tear you down.

Don't worry if you fail over and over again in this seven-day challenge. Eventually you will train your brain to automatically reject negative thoughts without even realising it.

I do that now myself. I have trained my brain to reject any negative thoughts without even thinking that I need to do it. Sometimes I find myself thinking of something negative, but my brain automatically says the word "erase" and I switch to positive. Over time I have anchored that word in my brain. Whenever I say it aloud now, my mind just switches.

If you can continue to meet this challenge, it will completely change your life. The world is full of negative, depressed people. You don't need to be like them. One of the major causes of depression is thinking negatively on a daily basis. You may think in a negative way just a little bit each day and then it grows to a lot each day, until you are depressed every day just thinking about all the things that could go wrong in your life.

Don't be this way. If you change, everything will change.

I hope that phrase has a major impact on your life. Remember that you are in control of your life. You don't need the rescue boat to come and save you, you can save yourself.

TWO

Once upon a time a king was travelling through the forest on the way home to his beloved castle. As he was passing through, he noticed that on some trees were painted red circles with arrows stuck right in the middle of the red circles. He continued on and saw many more trees like this, targets with arrows stuck in the middle of red painted circles.

The king was amazed and couldn't help but wonder who this amazing archer was, an archer who seemed to have an amazing eye and an amazing shot. The king approached a small village nearby and enquired about this incredible man.

The village folk said the archer was a man named Joe. The king at once requested to see this man.

A short time later, Joe was presented to the king and the king said, "Joe, you are an amazing archer, can I see you shoot an arrow and hit the target?" Joe at once got his bow and arrow out and pointed it at a tree nearby that had no red target.

Joe shot the arrow and hit the tree right in the middle. Then he grabbed his bag and reached in and took out some red paint and a brush. He then approached the arrow and painted a circle around it. The king was perplexed and asked Joe why he did this. Joe said, "I don't go and search for a target to hit. I just hit and then I create my target." The king shook his head and carried on with his journey.

Many people go through life searching for a target to hit and never end up finding one. They wait for circumstances, events to change, so that they can change. Little do they know that change may never come if they are constantly just waiting for it to come.

We must create our own targets, create our dreams, create our world, create our opportunities, create our goals, and create our life. If we just sit back and hope, then we will just keep getting the same things over and over again. People that are unstoppable realise that they create their own world. They realise that they have the power to create it.

The biggest tool that we all have for creating our life is the mind.

They say that the mind is the final frontier. Scientists are constantly amazed at the power of the brain and its ability to create. They say that we use maybe, at most, just five percent of our brain and with that five percent we have done amazing things.

Winston Churchill said that "you create your own universe as you go along."

I believe in a Creator and that we are a special creation and that we were created in the image of our Creator.

If we look around us and see this amazing planet, we cannot but be in awe of it and the Creator who created everything. If we were made in the Creator's image, then that means we are creators, we can create our world, our life, our dreams, and our goals. The best and only instrument to create these things is our mind.

Albert Einstein said, "Everything is energy and that's all there is to it. Match the frequency of the reality you want, and you cannot help but get that reality. It can be no other way. This is philosophy. This is physics."

What Einstein was saying is that everything is energy and everything is in constant movement. Let's look at an example. Next to me is a pen. If I look at this pen it appears solid, but if I take the pen and break it down, it is made up of atoms. If I go beneath the atoms, all I will find is pure energy constantly in motion.

This is what scientists have found, that the universe, when you break it down, is just pure energy. If you stood in front of a machine that shows the energy in objects, you would see on the screen that your whole body is aglow with energy. This is not some mystical thinking, it's science. They have broken down the atom and seen what it can do. Unfortunately, its power has also been used for horrendous weapons.

People may not believe that things attract each other. Each of us has the right to believe what we want, but there are many invisible things that we know are true and believe in, like electricity. I have no idea how electricity works but I do know it works. I cannot see the force of gravity, but if you jump out of an aeroplane gravity's force will pull you to the ground at a tremendous speed. It's the same with magnets; put a magnet near a small piece of metal and you will see the piece of metal move towards the magnet, a force that you cannot see but that you believe in.

The potential of the mind is just as impressive. We can't see it, but we know it's powerful.

Dr Dennis Waitley was a psychologist who worked with olympic athletes. Dr Waitley hooked the athletes up to machines and got them to run the race in their minds. He found that, as they were doing this, the muscles in their legs fired in exactly the same way as they were picturing them in their minds.

Their thoughts activated their muscles as if they were running the race. The mind can't distinguish between imagination and reality.

His conclusion was that if you can go there in the mind, you can go there in the body.

This is not some new thought. For centuries leaders have known the power of thinking and have kept the masses down by making sure they can have no hopes, goals, or dreams. Opium was once used to dull the minds of the people, because if they weren't drugged these people could have used the power of the mind to achieve great things in the world, and the leaders did not want this

Emerson said, "The ancestor of all action is thought."

When you look at people like Nelson Mandela,

Gandhi, Mother Teresa, and others like them, have you ever wondered how they could do the things that they did? They are no different from me and you; the only difference is that they realised the power of the mind.

Mother Teresa said that she would never go to an anti-war rally. She said if people had a peace rally, she would go, but not an anti-war rally.

Mother Teresa realised that if she thought war, she would get war. Even if the rally was anti-war, the part that the mind would focus on would be the war part.

This seems to be a problem for many people I meet on a day-to-day basis. They focus their minds on what they don't want. If they are focusing their mind on trying to get out of debt, the mind only sees debt, and that will keep bringing debt into their life. If they focus on not wanting to be alone, then they will always be alone. If the mind focuses on loneliness, then that is what it will attract into your life, like a magnet. If people want to get out of debt, they need to focus on having plenty of money, not debt. They need to set up a system where they can dig themselves out of debt and then focus on abundance. If they don't want to be lonely, then they should focus on what it feels like to have someone you can love in your life.

You see, you have to stop thinking of what you don't want and start thinking about what you do want.

You become what you think about because like attracts like. Your brain is like a magnet; whatever you focus on is what you will attract.

I already experienced this attraction before I understood it.

Thirteen years ago, when I started my first small business, some of my clients shut their businesses down and I lost them as clients. Without even realising it, I wasn't focusing on losing clients, I was focusing on getting more clients. Therefore, I got more clients, and this happened many times.

Another way I discovered this attraction was that I would notice that for some people, things just always went their way while for other people, things never went their way.

In their lives, they always had problems, one thing after another. I could never understand why this was. I never attributed it to bad luck. The difference was that some focused constantly on what they wanted and others always focused on what they did not want. You always get what you focus on, one way or another. So, always be careful of what you are thinking about, because if you really, really want something, you will get it and if you really, really don't want something, you will get that too.

Monitor your thoughts on a daily, hourly, and even minute-by-minute basis at times, because you will get whatever you focus on.

I remember when I first started driving in the country as a teenage boy, people used to say to me that when you're driving you shouldn't think about hitting the trees on the side of the road because if you're thinking about not hitting the trees, you might hit them.

You may say to yourself, "Oh no, I constantly think in a negative way." If you do, that's OK, because you can start changing the way you think in an instant and head in a new direction. The good thing is that a positive thought is much more powerful than a negative thought. If you are not sure exactly which way you are thinking, always be aware of how you are feeling.

Your feelings will tell you how you are thinking. If you are feeling a little fearful, unsure, scared, or worried, then you will attract things into your life that will keep you fearful, unsure, scared, or worried. But if you are feeling joyful, happy, content, blissful, or excited, then you will attract the things into your life that continue to make you joyful, happy, content, blissful, or excited.

You need to monitor your thoughts in real time like a pilot monitors the instruments in an aeroplane. He doesn't crash into the mountain and then a week later get the report of why he crashed. No, he knows how the plane is going at each moment. You don't want to crash and never realise why.

Monitor your thoughts so that you never crash. Your thoughts create your world. This may not be easy if you have never done it before. If you have always been reactive and not responsive, then it may take a little while to get comfortable.

When a pilot is flying a plane and the air is flowing evenly under and over the wings, the plane stays up in the sky. That is the law of lift. But if the pilot tilts the wings of the plane upwards, fast, the air cannot flow over the wings evenly and cannot keep the plane in the air, so it goes into a stall and just drops until it hits the ground. If the plane goes into a stall, the pilot has to go against his natural instinct to pull back on the steering controls to try and lift the plane, which would only make it worse. What he needs to do is a little bit uncomfortable. When the plane is in a stall, the pilot has to push the controls forward to push the nose of the plane down so the air flows evenly over and under the wings again and the law of lift kicks in.

When I go trail running, the tracks are well worn and easy to run on. If I wanted to take a new course and make a new track, the first time it wouldn't be easy, I would have to clear some branches, stomp down some grass, and move a few boulders, but the second time I ran that new track it would be a little easier and then the third time it would be even easier. The more times I run on that new track, the easier it gets.

Changing the way you think, from thinking what you don't want to thinking what you do want, may be a little uncomfortable at first, but before long you will find it easy to do and never think about what you don't want.

Thoughts are things. People become what they think about.

Ten years ago, just before I started personal development, I was in a severe motorbike accident. I wrote about this in my first book, *If You Change, Everything Will Change*.

I was on my motorbike and I got hit on the right side

of my body at high speed by a monster-sized vehicle. I flew through the air whilst unconscious. Upon landing in the middle of the road, both of my lungs were punctured by ten of my ribs that had completely fractured and I was struggling to breathe. I was brought to the hospital where they also discovered that my right arm was broken and I had a big contusion on the inside of my right leg and a few broken teeth. I was operated on because they needed to clean out my left lung. While in the hospital, I came down with a hospital virus which made me pretty sick. Despite all of this, I made a good recovery and was out of the hospital in thirty days.

The doctor overseeing me was amazed at my quick recovery. He attributed it to me being in good shape before the accident, but I knew differently. I knew it was my strong desire to get better and get back to normal as quickly as possible. Within two months of leaving the hospital, I was back at work running my business. When I left the hospital, my only thought was to get healthy. I focused on health, not on being sick and broken. There was no woe in my talk. I got back on track as quickly as my mind could get me there.

Always think of the good and not of what bad may come. You might say, "Well I have to think of the bad things that may come my way or I might not be prepared." That is true to an extent, but do you have to focus on it more than once?

For instance, if you are starting a new company, you may think just once that there is a chance that you may go bankrupt, but you only need to give this one thought and that's it. You don't need to keep thinking about bankruptcy. Think it once as an unlikely possibility and then give it no more thought whatsoever. Remember, the mind is a magnet, thoughts are things. You will attract whatever you are constantly thinking about.

One thing that I started doing a while ago is never reading, watching, or listening to the news. People may say that they need to be informed. That may be true to a very small extent, but do you really need to hear all the problems that are going on in the world? You can help the world without getting into its specific horrors. We know that there are starving kids in the world and we can help them and still have empathy without seeing pictures of dying children. If we keep focusing on starvation, then starvation is what we will always get.

The only reason the news media highlight all the terrible things in the world is because that is what pays. No news station would come on one night and say, "Tonight, we are telling you about all the great things happening in the world. We will show you acts of kindness and love. People being joyful. We will interview a family that are happy and all love each other and encourage each other. Then as we come to the end of the news, we will show you video footage of smiling children in Africa." That would be something I'd want to see!

How do most people start their day? They get up, go to the local café, and grab a coffee. While there, they look over and see the local paper. They grab it and start reading. They find out that a girl in the next suburb was raped and killed the night before. They are informed that there is a serial killer on the loose. They are informed that eighty-nine people were killed during a drone strike on a town in the Middle East. They are informed that an innocent bystander was dragged into a side alley and murdered. They are informed that there was a murder suicide in a family home and no one was left alive. They read all of these terrible things and then they go to work.

How do you think their day will go? What do you think they will attract into their lives?

Since I stopped the news from intruding into my life and put a stop to any negative thoughts coming into my mind, my life has been blissful, joyful, happy, and content and I always am in a positive state. Since I regularly monitor how I feel, when something unkind happens to me and I start to feel negative, I realise it before I crash and I start thinking positive thoughts that will attract positive things into my life.

Something I always say is that you should "Protect Happiness." True happiness is such a rare commodity and now that I have it, I protect it with my life. In my mind, I picture a soldier standing at the door to my mind and he lets nothing in that doesn't encourage happiness. Always guard the door to your mind, especially now that you realise that your thoughts have power.

There are so many benefits in positive thinking. One is your health. When you worry, think negatively, think of all the bad that could happen, you stress. Stress is a killer for humans. People who stress a lot die young. Stress just eats away at you. It eats away, not just at your mind but, when the stress hormone cortisol rises, at your whole body. When the mind is attacked, the body is attacked. Positive thinking helps the body to heal. Our cells replace themselves constantly. They say our whole body is replaced every month or so with new cells. Thinking healthy and not thinking unhealthy helps us improve our health.

Our thoughts are at the centre of all of this.

People become what they think about.

So, let's get a little specific and see how thinking can get us what we want.

The first step is knowing exactly what you want. Do you want to have lots of money? Do you just want good health? Do you want to live in a house by a lake and spend the rest of your life feeding the animals? Do you want to stay single or get married? Success means many different things to different people. I don't promote any particular lifestyle. I will show you how you can get the lifestyle you want, but it's up to you to decide which one you want.

Let's say that you want more money. You need to be specific on the amount. A goal I had many years ago was to make two hundred thousand dollars a year in income. This was not a great deal of money, but at that time it was the amount I wanted so I could freely travel the world. When I set that goal, I was making one hundred thousand dollars in income a year. This was just as I was starting to learn the power of goal setting. I reached my goal in less than a year.

So, let's say now you are making fifty thousand dollars a year and you want to make one hundred and fifty thousand dollars a year in income.

The first step is to focus your thoughts on the amount. Get a blank cheque and write the amount that you want on it. Write it to yourself and put it somewhere where you will see it every morning and every night. Get a picture of a pile of money in colour and write on the photo the amount you want. Your thoughts have to be focused on this amount throughout the day, so put this picture in your room, in the bathroom, in the kitchen, on the sun visor in your car.

When Jim Carrey first started his career, he wrote out a cheque to himself for ten million dollars and always looked at it. He went about his career believing that this money would come to him, and the rest is history. Visualisation plays such an important part.

The next step is a burning desire for this amount. If you are half-hearted about it, your mind will not attract it. To get a burning desire, you need to know what specifically you will do with the money. This is important. You need to know the specifics. When the money comes, how will it come? Cheque, cash, bank transfer? When it does come, how much will go to tax? How much will be put into savings? What debt will you pay off with this money?

You need to go through this process and make it clear. If I handed you the cheque today, what would you do with it? Which bank would you go to and deposit the cheque in? How many days will it take to clear?

You see what I mean about the specifics. When you think about it like this, it becomes real to you. When it becomes real to you, then your belief that you will get the amount you want goes up and your thoughts will attract it. I am not saying that this money will just appear. I don't believe that, but because you are thinking about it, things will happen in your life that you will notice and you will take action to put you in a position to earn the amount you want.

The next step is believing that you will get the money. If your amount was ten million dollars, that would be un-believable for most people and you need the amount to be believable.

Write your goal down on a piece of paper read what you have written day and night.

The next step is to picture yourself having already re-ceived the money. Feel the feelings of having the money, of spending it where you want to spend it. Day and night close your eyes and feel the joy of already having the money. Throughout the day, think of this money and what it is like having received it.

The last step is to feel happy now. You must control how you think and how you feel so that throughout the day you are in a happy state. If you are focusing on your amount in an unhappy state, your thoughts will never work to get the amount you want. Thoughts and feelings play the biggest part in all of this.

The main thing is that you believe that the universe is on your side and wants to help you. You need to be open to any way that the universe will do this.

Maybe in your current job it is not possible. The universe may then show you a way to get another job. Maybe you will notice things that will lead you to start your own business as a vehicle for the money to come to you.

You can't just sit in the corner and wait. The money can only come through the universe providing different opportunities for it to come to you. You may meet a new client, you may get a new business deal. There are so many ways the universe might channel this money to you. Your job is to take the opportunity once it arrives.

The important thing is not to worry about the 'how' – how it will come about. That's not your role; just believe it will come.

Life will pay whatever price you ask. You just have to know how to ask. Earl Nightingale many years ago had an audio program called *The Strangest Secret*. The strangest secret was that you become what you think about. Whatever you focus on is what you will get. Constantly think of positive things and you will get positive things. Constantly think about negative things and you will get negative things.

Nightingale said that this was the strangest secret because it is all around us but no one is consciously using it. It's around us and many don't even realise it. It's not a secret at all, but very few people use it.

I was at the airport the other day and I was talking

to a young man who wanted to become a comedian or a comedy writer for a TV program. I was giving him some advice and he said that my material would be very good for his friend who is unsuccessful. As soon as he started to talk about his friend, guess what? His phone rang. Who was it? The very friend he was talking to me about and more importantly, thinking about. Has this happened to you? I love it when that happens, because it happens to me too often to just be a coincidence.

I have attracted everything I have ever wanted into my life. All my goals have been realised and the new dreams I have are all coming true. I attract only good and positive things into my life because I am always thinking positive. You can too!

Start small, start with you. Training your mind does not happen overnight, but it does happen. Start with changing how you act, how you feel, get immersed in personal development and acquire success habits. Read the books, go to the seminars, study yourself, and see the changes take place before your very eyes.

Life can be challenging, but the universe is on your side. Yes, the universe will test you at times, but it wants to see if you have the ability to control your thoughts. When the universe tests you, say the things I say to the universe.

I say to the universe, "My dear Universe, I don't take you seriously. I know that you are on my side. I know that you test me and that you throw challenges my way from time to time, but when you do I just laugh. You do give joy and happiness to me and for this I am forever grateful but you, yes you, are sneaky. You test my resolve to remain happy and joyful despite circumstances. So, when you challenge me, I turn to laughter, laughter that you think you could ever get me, but that you do keep trying. The more you try, the more I laugh, because I have no time for tears, only rejoicing. I use my laughter to turn problems into solutions. You bring people into my life and then you take them away, you trickster. You know before bringing these people into my life, that I will reject them because of their negative courses. You can be devious at times, but I keep winning because I know that in your heart, Mr Universe, you love me. I keep winning because I can think my own thoughts, in a place that you cannot control no matter how hard you try. Mr Universe, I tip my hat to you for a life of fun, joy, and laughter, thank you."

Please don't use the power of thought for any harm. We see evil dictators use this power for evil. They focus on evil and hatred, so that is what comes into their lives and they become very good at being evil.

When Andrew Carnegie was a small boy, he wrote his life goal on a piece of paper. He wrote that he wanted to use the first half of his life to accumulate money and the last half of his life to give it all away. This he did. He became the richest man in the world at the beginning of the twentieth century, but he had a problem when it came to giving his money away because he wanted his wealth to be used in a good and positive way, not in evil ways. One of the great things I speak and write a lot about is how Carnegie used his money to open libraries across the United States of America. He wanted everyone to be able to learn regardless of their economic circumstances.

So please, use your mind for good. Think only about positive things, leave the negative things to those who are negative. Please remember to feel good now. This is so important. Life is a wonderful adventure, so join me on this journey. Gratitude is something you should feel every day.

In 1999, Roberto Benigni won an Oscar for his movie *Life is Beautiful*. For me, this was the best Oscar moment in history. In his speech, Roberto thanked his parents for giving him the best gift, the gift of poverty. Roberto Benigni is one of the most grateful people I have encountered. After poverty, he is so grateful for everything he has today.

Every morning when you wake up, be grateful for all the good things in your life. Be grateful that you have received this special gift, life.

You are a special creation; your brain is magnificent. Believe that you can achieve anything. Your wish is your command. Whatever it is that you want in life, believe without a doubt that you will get it. Belief is the foundation of success. Believe that you can do it and the 'how' will come your way.

Don't settle just for existence. I was speaking to a young man recently and he said that he doesn't mind being grumpy every now and again. How sad is that?

That he has gotten himself to the point where he is comfortable with feeling bad. He is trapped. He has found comfort in misery.

We don't ever want to become that way. If we are there now, then we should want to get out of that state right away. Being OK with misery is like a dog lying down on the ground making a low uncomfortable moan. A passer-by says to the dog's owner, "Why is the dog moaning?" The man replies, "He is resting on a small nail." The passer-by then asks, "Why doesn't he just get up and move?" The owner responds, "Because it doesn't hurt him that much."

Never settle for a life that is not completely full of joy and happiness. If we say to ourselves that life is hard, then it will be hard. If we tell ourselves that life is easy, then it will be that way too.

Never settle for second best. Life is a marvellous adventure.

In life you will be able to do the things that people say are impossible to do. They may laugh at first, but they won't laugh in the end. Keep your goals and dreams to yourself and only share them with people who will encourage you and build you up. You can have, do, or be anything you want. Follow your bliss and the universe will open the doors for you to succeed. Remember the young archer I spoke about at the beginning of this chapter. Create your own target. Create your own bullseye, create your own dreams, create your own life. As the creator of your own destiny, imagine what you can do from now on.

THREE

In the year 1883, a man was born who would forever change the minds of businessmen around the world. His name was Napoleon Hill.

Napoleon started his career as a journalist and one day he was given the assignment of interviewing the richest man in the world. His name was Andrew Carnegie. Carnegie was the boss of the steel industry in the US.

Carnegie liked the way Hill conducted himself in the interview, so he invited him to spend a few days at his home. During that stay, Carnegie offered Hill the chance of a lifetime. Carnegie asked Hill if he wanted to undertake an assignment. The assignment was to spend the next twenty years interviewing all the wealthy and successful men in America to distill the secret of their success.

Carnegie was not going to pay him for this work. Hill was to do it all on his own. Carnegie said he would give Hill letters of introduction so he would be in a position for these men to teach him all that they knew about being successful. After twenty years of research, interviews, firsthand lessons, and experiences, Hill wrote a book about all that he had learned.

It wasn't until he had completed the book that he came up with the title of the book. The publisher was pressuring him for a title and before he went to bed one night, he asked his subconscious to come up with a million-dollar title.

The next morning Hill arose, with the title *Think and Grow Rich* firmly entrenched in his mind.

This book has sold over 100 million copies since the time it was written at the beginning of last century. In this book is the secret that very few people know and, when they read the book, many people believe that the steps which the book asks the reader to take will not work. Therefore, they don't become successful.

The ones who do believe the book and take action, go on to become extremely successful.

I won't tell you the specifics of the book because that will be for you to find out when you get your copy, but I will tell you how I've applied what the book says and how I continue to apply it in my life.

The book is based on making lots of money, but it can be applied to every aspect of your life. I don't necessarily advocate people being rich. It is up to you how you would like to live your life, but the book's principles can be applied to your health, your family, other relationships, your business, or to making money.

Success is a formula. If you spent time with a pastry chef and he told you to get a piece of paper out and watch him very carefully and write down every single step he takes in making a beautiful chocolate cake and write down all the ingredients that he puts in the cake, even down to the last gram, and write down how he bakes it and for how long, you will be able to make that chocolate cake taste exactly the way the pastry chef intended it to taste.

You see, there's a formula for making a beautiful chocolate cake. What would happen if you then took those notes you wrote down and followed the recipe as close as you could, but you left out one or two ingredients? Would the cake come out the same as it did when the chef made it? Absolutely not.

Napoleon Hill found out what the formula for success was and he told the world about his discovery, but unfortunately many people didn't follow it. Of the ones who did, some took out key ingredients. The ones who followed the recipe exactly got massive results.

It's up to you how you want to apply the formula for success. Success is the ongoing realisation of a worthy ideal. If you want to make a million dollars and you work towards that goal, then you are a success. If you want to live off a farm in the mountains, then you are a success. If you want to be a professional piano player or maybe get a job in a particular field that you enjoy or raise a family, as long as you are progressing towards your goal you are a success.

I will show you the formula for success that I have applied.

It all starts in the mind. The book Hill wrote was titled *Think and Grow Rich*, not 'invest and grow rich' or 'buy houses and grow rich', but *Think and Grow Rich*.

Success starts in the mind. It is how you use your mind on a daily basis that will determine if you are successful or not. People who are happy and successful have learnt how to use their brain in the right way. What's the difference between two people who live in the same city? One may be happy and successful while another is getting kicked out of their home and is unsuccessful and unhappy, but the thing that all the successful people agree on is that the difference is in the person's mind and how they use it. It's the thoughts they have.

So here is the formula for success.

Step One

You have to specifically define what your goal is. If I asked you today what your goals for your future were and you couldn't tell me specifically within three seconds, then you don't know what you want or, at least, you haven't defined what you want. You may have an idea of what you want but the idea is not specific. You should be able to rattle it off straightaway. Let's take the goal of a new car as an example.

You may tell me that you want a new car. The specifics are: What type of car? What colour? What make and model? What engine power? What does the interior look like? What is the colour and fabric of the interior? How many doors does the car have? How many seats? What is the brand of the tyres?

You see, this is specific regarding your goal. If you

can get all that you want clear in your mind, then that's a start. If you shrug your shoulders and say that you don't know what you want, the universe will be behind you shrugging its shoulders because it doesn't know what to bring you.

If it is fitness goals, what weight do you want to be at? How much muscle do you want? How far do you want to be able to run? How many sit-ups do you want to be able to do? How much weight do you want to lift? How many calories do you want to consume in a day? What sort of foods do you want to eat to help your body get to where you want it to be?

If it is relationship goals, whom do you want to spend time with? Why do you want to spend time with them? What do you want to do more with them? How much kindness, love, and respect do you want to give them on a regular basis? The list goes on.

If it is a monetary figure, how much do you want to earn? When would you like to have this money? What is the specific dollar figure? Is a cheque coming to you or a bank transfer, or do you want it at regular intervals until you reach your figure?

Can you see the difference between having a vague idea and a specific idea of what you want? All successful people know exactly want they want, how they want it, and even why they want it. Spend time and think about your goals and write down the specifics.

People have said to me that they don't know what they want. If this is true for you, then find out what you really want by taking fifteen minutes to sit down some-where quiet and go over different life scenarios in your mind. When you are thinking of different life possibili-ties, take note of the ones that make you smile and the ones that make you feel happy. Generally, these are the things that you will want in life because the thing that all people want is to be happy.

Step Two
You have to believe that you can achieve your goal. You need faith in its fulfilment.

If you don't believe that it's possible for you to achieve your goal, then you won't achieve it. You have to believe to achieve.

If you say to yourself that you want to make twenty million dollars in the next two years and you now only make twenty thousand dollars a year, that goal might be unbelievable for you, so that's not a good goal to choose.

You have to find your sweet spot. The spot where the goal both excites you and you believe that you can achieve it, whether it is monetary or otherwise.

If you believe it, you will put all your effort and thinking into achieving your goal and that's why you will achieve it. If you don't really believe it will happen, you will put in very little effort and you won't use your best thinking abilities to achieve it, so therefore you won't believe and achieve.

Step Three

What are you willing to give for your goals to become reality?

There is no such thing as something for nothing. What can you give in order to get your goal? You cannot just sit in the corner and wait for a knock at the door for someone to hand you success, you need to take action in some area. If you are not sure, then just start somewhere and things will tend to pop up in your life. Your brain then tends to start seeing things that were always there, but which you just didn't realise were there.

Recently my mother was talking to me about getting a new car. She told me the make and model that she wanted. The next morning, I was driving along a road that I drive on every day and there it was on a massive billboard, the exact car my mother wanted. That billboard had been up for a while and I had seen it, but I hadn't really noticed it. Your brain cannot take conscious notice of every little thing because you would go crazy. A lot of things stay in the subconscious. It wasn't until I specifically thought about the car that I noticed it right in front of my eyes.

So, if you have clear goals in mind, things will start to pop up that were always there but now you will become conscious of them.

Step Four

You have to have a burning desire to achieve your goals.

It must burn inside of you enough to keep you up

all night and get you up early in the morning to achieve those goals. If you are just thinking that it would be nice if I reached my goals or if it happens great and if it doesn't happen then that's OK too, then it will never happen. It has to drive you. You will know it's a burning desire because of how you go about your day. If you go about it timidly playing it safe, then it is not a burning desire. You cannot get to second base with your foot on first base.

Burn your bridges; this is it, you will never go back. That's how you know it's a burning desire, because you give it your all. You can't sit in front of the TV each night for hours on end and achieve your goals at the same time.

Step Five
Write down on a piece of paper a statement of what you want. Every night and every morning, read aloud your statement. You need your statement to be clear to both parts of your brain, the conscious and the subconscious, so if your conscious mind is not thinking about it, then your subconscious mind is.

Step Six
This step is very important. Throughout the day you need to feel the feelings that you would have if you had already achieved your goal. How would that feel? Picture yourself sitting in that new car and feel those feelings. Picture yourself sitting with a loved one and talking, feel those feelings. Picture yourself with one million dollars

in your bank account, feel those feelings. Throughout the day, dream, dream as if all that you want has just happened, has all come true, that you are there and you have done it. Your goal has come true, congratulations, your wish is now a reality; feel those feelings.

You cannot be a millionaire if you cannot feel what it's like to be a millionaire.

The steps that I have outlined are not difficult at the start. The hard part comes when you try to sustain these steps over a long period of time, but If you are sincere and determined, you will. These steps are easy to take but also easy not to take. That's where the burning desire comes into play, to keep you going through the hard times.

Reasons play a major role in achieving success. If you don't have really strong reasons to accomplish your goals, there is a good chance that you won't.

What are your reasons for wanting to become successful? If you have strong enough reasons, they will pull you through the difficult moments.

I will give you myself as an example.

My reason for writing this book is the fact that I know the principles in it can change people's lives for the better, as they have for me. That is my reason. That is why I started my education company. My goal is always to help people.

In my personal life, it is my spirituality that I try to help people with. In my business career, it's helping people to live happy successful lives which gets me up in the morning, ready to go. This is why I travel around the world. The funny thing is that helping people is my main goal, but money seems to come my way too. Zig Ziglar said that if you help enough people get what they want, then you will get everything you want.

Jim Rohn had a word that he loved, and I love it as well. It is the word "until." Keep applying the principles I have talked about until you become successful, until you become unstoppable.

Have you ever tried to stop an ant going in the direction it is heading? If you put something in its way, the ant tries to go to the left. If that doesn't work, the ant will try and go to the right. If that doesn't work, the ant will try and go over and then it will try and dig a tunnel to go under. In the end, the ant will try and burrow through the obstacle because one thing that the ant will not do is quit. It keeps going until it succeeds.

I would like you to be exactly the same way. Never give up on reaching your goals. This is what will make you unstoppable.

Successful people don't give up. They keep going until they achieve their aim in life. It's the ones who stop after six months, a year, or two years who remain unsuccessful. Do it or die trying, that's the resolve I wish for you.

Don't listen to people who say that you won't be able to achieve your goals. Even well-meaning family members or friends might be negative. Even though you love them, don't believe in their beliefs. When I started my company, I had no doubt that I was going to succeed. When I spoke to my friends, they were very doubtful. They were telling me, "Well, if it doesn't work, you can do something else." In their minds they could only see the barriers directly in front of me, whereas I could see all the way to the end goal and being unsuccessful never entered my mind because I was unstoppable.

For people who understand this, no explanation is required and for those who don't understand, no explanation will suffice.

Don't listen to people's negative talk. Be resolved, resolute, unchanging, don't go back.

Don't take advice from unsuccessful people, whether you are close to them or not.

Find out what unsuccessful people read and don't read it. Find out where unsuccessful people go and don't go there. Find out what unsuccessful people say and don't say it.

People constantly think about what they don't want. That is wrong thinking. It should be changed to thinking about what you do want.

Using your time wisely is such an important thing when you have goals to reach. Don't be like the average American, who watches TV for five hours a day. What a waste of time and life. A little TV watching is fine when it is used to rest your mind and body, but not to just entertain yourself at the expense of reaching your goals.

Don't follow the crowd. It's sad to say, but the majority of people either don't have goals or are not working to achieve them. Success can be had by everyone because we all want to be successful in different areas of our life.

A warning about not doing what everyone else does appeared in my life a few years ago.

I had a young man working for me, a great guy who wanted to become a firefighter. In the state of Victoria, every year the Metropolitan Fire Brigade asks people to go online on a certain day at a certain time to fill in an online application for that year's very limited number of positions in the Brigade. Apparently, because of the sheer number of online applicants, the site often crashes and that's what happened to my friend. He filled out all his details and just before he was ready to submit his form, his internet page crashed and he did not get in.

He did what everyone else did and it didn't work.

What I would have done would have been totally different. At least a year before I could fill out the online application form, I would spend as much time as I could at a local fire station. I would get to know the firefighters, I would wash the trucks, sweep the floors, and get involved as much as I could as a friendly neighbourhood volunteer. I would have gotten involved in the local charities which the station runs. Basically, I would have spent as much time as possible with the organisation so that when the time came for applications, I would never have had to even go online. They would have already known me and seen that I was willing to do whatever it takes to be a firefighter.

Yes, this would have taken up a lot of my time,

but who cares, this is my burning desire. I would have thought of nothing else but becoming a firefighter.

This is an example of not following the crowd, not doing what everyone else does. You have to think of what you want and eliminate any thought of not being able to achieve your goals.

I go after things with passion and a knowledge that I cannot fail. How else would I go about my goals? Unless someone can prove with real hard evidence that it's impossible for me to be successful, then I will act as if success will come my way one way or another.

Viktor Frankl spoke about his chances of surviving the concentration camps. He said it was a twenty-nine to one shot that he would get out alive. Although he knew that, unless anyone could prove to him that he could not survive, he was going to continue thinking that he would survive, and survive he did.

Jim Carrey once talked about his father in a commencement speech. He said that his father could have been a great comedian but, because he didn't believe it was possible for him, he took a safe job as an accountant. But after a time he was let go from that job and the family suffered. His father failed at what he didn't want to do, so you might as well take your chances at what you love.

I completely agree that if you can fail at things you don't really want in life, then you should go for your dreams and believe that you will attain them until someone can prove otherwise.

The great thing about starting down the road towards

your goals is that once you pick up some momentum, things just start happening. I don't know how or why this happens; it just does.

When you have two teams playing basketball, as soon as one team gets two, three, or even four baskets in a row while the other team gets none, then the team with no baskets will immediately call a time-out because they know the danger and power of momentum. If the coach doesn't quickly put a brake on that momentum, he could be down twenty points in a matter of minutes. That is the power of momentum; when a few things start happening, other things just seem to fall into place. This is another reason that you should not give up, because this vital momentum could kick in at any moment.

Make a resolution to yourself that you will not quit on reaching your goals and becoming successful and unstoppable. When you make an internal resolution and stick to it, you give your brain the command that failure is not an option and that it had better get to work on making your goals come true.

Be persistent, like an ant. It doesn't matter what comes up in your life, you will succeed or die trying.

FOUR

It was 1945 and the end of one of the most horrific times in human history. The evil march of Germany through Europe was finally over, but one thing that the Allied forces did not yet realise was the horror that the German army and SS had inflicted even deep within their own borders. They discovered concentration camps with the purpose of eliminating the Jewish race. As Allied troops entered these camps for the first time, often filming as they did so, true evil showed its ugly face. All they saw were the remains of what were once human beings and people who were spared death but were barely alive and missing their humanity.

In of one of these camps was my hero, Viktor Frankl.

Frankl was an Austrian psychiatrist who was sent to the concentration camp at Auschwitz. In camp life he witnessed firsthand how men surviving in the camp didn't lose their humanity. He noticed an existential vacuum in those prisoners who had no hope. When they lost their hope, they soon died.

He is my hero because of how he was able to control his thinking while in the camp. His book was one of the most important things I ever read and it changed my life. A quote from Frankl I will never forget and that I continue to study to this day is, "Between stimulus and response, there is a space. In that space is our power to choose our response. In our response lies our growth and our freedom."

I would like to continue to talk about these words because if you can really extract the meaning of these words, you can completely change your life.

Frankl was saying that the stimulus is what happens to us, either internal or external. The response is what we do about what has happened to us. He was saying that between the two, stimulus and response, there is a space. In this space we have what he called the "last human freedom" to choose how we will respond.

When they were doing horrific things to Frankl, they could take away everything he owned and he could only stand there naked, but one thing that they could not take away from him was his last human freedom, his choice, his attitude to what was happening to him. That was a decision, a choice, that only he could make. He couldn't do anything about what was happening to him, so all he could control was his attitude to what was happening to him. In that space between stimulus and response he could choose his response and no one could take that away from him. They could take away every possession he owned, but they could not take away his humanity, only he could make that choice, the choice whether he would keep it or let it be stolen from him.

In the camp he saw this humanity in other prisoners. There were ones who gave their last piece of bread away to help another prisoner. Frankl said, "Everything can be taken from a man except the last of human freedoms, to choose one's attitude in any given circumstances, to let those rob you of your very self, your inner freedom."

The reason why I say that if you can really think about this, it will change your life, is because you will discover your inner freedom, a freedom that no one can ever take away from you. It can be in small matters or in big matters.

Here are a few examples, let's say someone you know one day tells you all the things they don't like about you (the stimulus.) Before you respond to them or respond internally to their words you have a space where you can choose how you will respond. Will you just react, or will you use that space to choose your response? Will you let them take away your dignity, your humanity?

If a doctor gives you some medicine, the worst thing that could happen to you is having a reaction to it. The best thing is if you respond to the medicine, not react to it.

It is the same with us; never just react, choose your response, use that last human freedom you have, that freedom which no one can take away from you.

If your boss calls you into the office and yells at you, choose your attitude and your response. If your spouse does something that annoys you, choose your attitude and your response. If you lose all your money, choose your attitude and choose your response. If you are falsely charged with a crime, choose your attitude and choose your response. If you are struck with a physical impediment, choose your attitude and choose your response.

You have this last human freedom, no one can take it away from you, and if you applied it to every situation in your life, your life would change.

This might not be easy to do at the start, but if you keep doing it you will start doing it automatically.

If you've read my first book, *If You Change, Everything Will Change*, you would have read about my severe motorbike accident that nearly killed me and nearly left me paralysed.

In my recovery I used my last human freedom. I couldn't change what had happened to me, all I could change was my attitude to what had happened to me, and from that time forward my life changed.

An interesting thing that Frankl noticed in the camp was how people dealt with suffering.

Do you ever suffer? Maybe from the death of a loved one or a tragic circumstance that you cannot change, maybe a medical condition that cannot be cured. It could be anything that is out of your control, a situation of despair.

In an interview, Frankl talked about despair. He said that despair equals suffering without meaning. If a man cannot find any meaning in his suffering, he will be prone to despair. Once he can see a meaning to his suffering, he can turn his tragedy into a personal human triumph. He can only do this if he puts meaning to his suffering.

That is why I can honestly say to you that I don't suffer, because when a tragedy hits I straightaway put meaning into that tragedy and into my life. When my father passed, it was a time of suffering, but it did not last long because I put meaning into that suffering, and that is why the suffering did not turn into despair. I put meaning into my father's life and into my life going forward. I look to the future and put meaning into what I now do and what my father would want me to do and I celebrate his life instead of continuing to mourn his loss.

Frankl, a psychiatrist said, "Suffering ceases to be suffering when it finds meaning in the fact that the suffering is unavoidable." If we can avoid suffering, then of course we try to avoid it, but if it is unavoidable and we put real meaning to it, it can be changed from suffering to a triumph.

Can you see how powerful it is to take control of your mind and know that you have the ability to do so? It is liberating to know that no matter what happens to you or what anyone does to you, they cannot take away your humanity, they cannot control how you think. That is true freedom.

In the camp, Frankl noticed that the ones who died quickly were the ones without hope for the future. Once someone lost their view of the future and what good things it could bring, they would not survive for long. The body would either give out and die or they would take their own life by running into the electrified fence. The ones who looked to the future with a goal in mind were the ones who survived.

The ones who had a dream, a hope, something to do once they were liberated from the camp, had a higher chance of survival, whether it was a book to finish or a family member to embrace, hope had kept them from losing their humanity.

Frankl pictured himself in a lecture hall, lecturing to students on what he was learning in the camp. This future dream helped him survive. He who has a 'why' to live for, can deal with any 'how'.

So, no matter what happens to you, put meaning to it and have something in the future that you are looking forward to.

When the USS Indianapolis was sunk by a German U-boat, the crew were in the water for days. Everybody at some point wanted to give up, but those around him would help him look towards the future, the family he would see again, the things he would do after his rescue, and even his children not born yet.

The men put meaning to their suffering, the meaning of their survival. The meaning that if they died, what would that mean for the loved ones who would miss them dearly?

We might not go through something as bad as a sinking ship, but if thinking this way works under such tragic circumstances, it will work even for all the little sufferings in our own life. What doesn't kill you, will make you stronger. I'm sure you have heard that saying.

People often ask what the meaning of life is, and they often cannot figure it out. What they should ask, is what is life asking back from me? This is a great question when we are facing trials, because if we are constantly asking life to do something for us, it might all be in vain, but if we ask what we can do for life, we can change our attitude from waiting to now acting.

John F. Kennedy said, "Do not ask what your country can do for you, ask what you can do for your country."

If we are waiting on life to help us, then we have failed. Life will only help us if we try to help life.

If it's not physical action, it can be mental action. We control our brains, no one can take that from us. Whatever tragedies you are facing in life, please use what Frankl said and turn tragedy into personal triumph.

No one can take away the life experience you have when you are dealing with trying situations. Will you lose the experience you have learnt or forget about it? Gather all the experiences that you have stored all your life and use them.

This is what Frankl did when he was liberated from the camp. He put what he had learned in the camps to good use, he continued his work as a psychiatrist and became head of the neurology department at the Polyclinic in Vienna. He developed the practice of logotherapy. The Greek word *logos* means reason and logotherapy is built on the premise that the primary motivation of an individual is to find meaning in life.

One thing I admire about Frankl was that after he was liberated from the camp, he was not looking for vengeance. The SS guards did unspeakable things to their prisoners, but vengeance was not on his mind. He said that no one has the right to do wrong even if wrong has been done to them. This is also scriptural advice that goes back thousands of years and it is something that I try to apply. If I start to want "payback", I stop myself and realise that I have the space between stimulus and response and I can use that space to change my attitude to any individual or to any circumstance.

Since I became an entrepreneur, I have read many books. Recently I was reading a book from a very well-known businessman. In the book, the man goes on and on about how, if someone has done you wrong, then you need to get back at them. It was all about payback. I think that is completely wrong.

If a man like Victor Frankl, a man who had evil atrocities committed on him and had many reasons for vengeance, did not seek revenge, then we never should. Victor Frankl was a man of character.

In camp life, Frankl said, it wasn't the beatings that hurt the most. it was the injustice and unreasonableness of it all, that was what really hurt. One day during a work assignment, Frankl was leaning on his shovel and not working and a top SS guard noticed this. The guard didn't beat him, as was the usual punishment, but instead he picked up a stone and threw it at him, just as you would call a dog over to you.

It was the indignity of it all, being treated like an animal. But despite of it all, Frankl decided what his attitude would be.

One thing that Frankl talks a lot about is decisions.

We make them every day, both small and large decisions.

You decide with ease what to wear on any given day, what to eat, what to do that day etc. What about when it comes to the big decisions in life? Sometimes, we can become very hesitant, to the point where we make no decision at all. We decide not to decide or we analyse a decision so much that we suffer from the paralysis of analysis.

What about if you ignored all the conditions around your decisions, affirming that no matter the conditions you will make the right decisions? Deciding what you want to become and where you want to go and what you want to do should be like that.

Make decisions despite the circumstances, because if you wait for the 'right' circumstances to come, you may be waiting all your life. So, decide, I want to become this or I want to become that, despite the circumstances. The perfect circumstances might not be there, but your freedom to choose your response to life means you can decide where you want to go and just go, no matter what the circumstances. If you want to start a company, then just decide to do it, no matter what. If you want a loving relationship, then attract a loving relationship. If you want better health, then decide that's what you want and go get it. This is human greatness at work, that no matter what the circumstances are, we can decide.

If it is success that you are after, don't chase success. If it is happiness that you are after, then don't chase happiness. Chase the things that can bring success and happiness to you and give yourself over to them no matter what you want, and these things will bring themselves into your life. If you just chase happiness, you will never catch it. It will become like a butterfly that you cannot catch, but if you chase things that can make you happy then happiness will bring itself into your life.

Have you ever tried to chase a cat? What normally happens? The cat scrambles away and is very hard to catch. But if you stop trying to catch it and just sit on the couch, what usually happens? The cat will find you and sit on your lap.

I am not talking about goals, because these are very important, and I will discuss goals later. I am talking about people chasing the feelings of happiness, the feelings of success, because these will be fleeting if we just go after them alone. We should go after the things that can bring these feelings into our lives. For example, I would never try and chase romantic love, because I would never get it. What I would do if I wanted a romantic relationship, is to find a girl with beautiful qualities who treats me, other people, and herself well and once I find her and spend time with her, then the feeling of love will arrive without me chasing it.

Decide what you want and go after it. If it is feelings, then go for the things that can bring those feelings.

Please remember that you have the freedom to decide and no one can take that from you.

I often wonder how I would have fared in Auschwitz. Life where, when you went to get your one daily meal, you hoped that the Capo (prisoner in charge) would lower his ladle to the bottom of the pot so he could scoop out a few peas for you instead of scooping from the top where it would only be hot water. Would I have run into the electric fence? Would I have tried to escape? Would I have been bitter about life? Would I have tried to seek revenge against the SS guards? I would like to think that I would have acted like Frankl and seen the opportunity to turn this suffering into a personal human triumph.

How would you have acted? Why not start applying these things in your life today, so that no matter what the future brings, you will be victorious?

Please study the sentence, "Between stimulus and response, you have the freedom to choose your response."

Victor Frankl died in 1997 at the ripe old age of 92. He died with his humanity and his dignity intact.

FIVE

In 1962, before a cheering crowd, US President John F. Kennedy gave a speech. In that speech he said, "We choose to go to the moon in this decade and do the other things, not because they are easy but because they are hard."

On July 20th, 1969, a man stepped onto the moon, an achievement beyond compare. From the moment President Kennedy set a goal on behalf of his nation, that one clear focus was to walk on the moon, and walk on the moon they did.

We all want things in life, and one person's goals are very different from another person's goals. That is what makes the experience of goal setting a personal and maybe a private one.

I would love for you to do something. The next time you sit down for a coffee or a tea, take out a piece of paper and write your story. Not about your life thus far, but your life from this day on.

Start it like this – Once a upon a time…– and write your life story, not starting from days past, but from this day forward. Write about where you want to live. What you want to have. Where you want to go. With whom you want to go. How much money you want. What sort of health you want. What you want to feel. Write page after page and just let your mind come up with whatever you want to do, to be, or to have.

What would be the perfect life for you? You may have already done this in your head, but I would guess that you have not written the whole story in your head yet. There is something about putting pen to paper that makes a huge difference. Tell the story like it is a fairytale that will come true.

Once you have done that, take out another piece of paper and break down your dreams into specific points. Set one-year goals, five-year goals, ten-year goals. What do you want to do?

Where do you want to go? One day you need to stand right in front of the Colosseum in Rome and just be in awe. You have to eat the finest tapas in Barcelona, and I can tell you about the nicest views in southern France.

How much weight do you want to lose? Goals such as walking or running each day. Drinking a glass of green juice every morning. Eating healthy etc.

How much do you want to earn? Maybe starting your own business. Investing your money. It could be that you want to become a multimillionaire.

Whom do you want to spend more time with? It could be spending more time with certain friends or family members. It could be to find the love of your life. You may want to marry and have children.

What sport would you like to play more? Maybe there's a certain hobby you would like to take up.

There are emotional goals like being happy every day, smiling more. Finding the good in people instead of the bad.

The list of goals goes on and on, but when it is down in writing, you can look at it every day and work towards your goals. The feeling of crossing goals that you have reached off your list is a fantastic feeling.

Once you have your goals down, then go through my success formula in Chapter Two and use that to achieve your goals.

Be very specific about your goals. Get a burning desire for the achievement of your goals. Write out on a separate piece of paper your one-year goals and read them out day and night. Believe that you can reach your goals. Feel the feelings as if you have already achieved your goals and be happy right now.

Once upon a time, two men were sitting on their boat a mile offshore from Escape Island. They were looking at the island that they were approaching, when suddenly they saw a man running out of the jungle with chains around his hands. Once the man reached the shoreline, he jumped into a small boat with no sails up. The man tried to row but the waves kept knocking him back into the rocks. He tried and tried, but the end result was the same; he kept hitting the rocks.

Not being able to get away, this man was recaptured by his captors. One of the two men watching this all unfold asked the other, "What happened, why could he not get away? Was the current too strong for him to row?" The other man turned to him and said, "The problem was he was trying with all his strength, but he didn't know how to use the sail. The wind and the waves just knocked him around and in the end he got nowhere. If he had just put his sail up, the wind would have taken him in the direction that he wanted to go in."

Many people are like this escapee. They know they want to go somewhere and to change their life, but they have not set their sail, so they get knocked around by life and its circumstances and end up going nowhere.

If we want to achieve our dreams and our goals, then we need to put up a sail. We need to know exactly the direction we want to go in and it doesn't matter which way the wind blows, we will never hit the rocks and always reach our destination.

Keep your goals firmly in mind, believe that you can have them. Feel those feelings of accomplishment and you will achieve them.

SIX

On May 29th 1953, Sir Edmund Hilary and Nepalese Sherpa and mountaineer Tenzing Norgay reached their goal. They set out to accomplish something remarkable and were determined to accomplish what they had set out to do.

The two men were tired, sore, and alone, but in just a few more steps, they would accomplish something that no other man had ever accomplished. They had reached the summit of the tallest mountain in the world; they could see a view that no one had ever seen while standing on Earth. These men conquered Mt Everest; what an achievement, what a feat of pure determination. They would go down in the history books for this great accomplishment. For the rest of their lives, they could reflect on this moment.

As Sir Edmund so eloquently put it, "People do not decide to become extraordinary, they decide to accomplish extraordinary things."

These men were persistent and determined and that meant that they would never give up on the achievement of their goal.

These two qualities of persistence and determination

are very important if we want to have an extraordinary life. As the saying goes, you don't have to do extraordinary things in life, just do ordinary things extraordinarily well and then you'll be extraordinary.

That means never giving up, even when difficult times come, and they will come. It would be a perfect world if problems never came into our lives. We have sunshine and we have rain and every now and again we have a freak storm.

These things cannot be avoided, but if you implement the principles I have mentioned in this book, then you can overcome any challenge, even the freak storms of life.

Persistence and determination are just words to some people, but to many others they are the driving force of their lives.

That means never giving up, no matter what life throws at us. Are you prepared if life throws a major challenge your way? What if you were called upon to save the lives of hundreds of people or possibly thousands? Would fear take control of you and render you helpless? Or would you push aside all fear and trepidation and be determined to do whatever needs to be done?

Unfortunately, fear plays a major role in the lives of many who are crippled by this feeling. They become scared to do anything that is not in their comfort zone and therefore they never grow.

For me, fear is an ally not an enemy. Fear is like a soldier who whispers in my ear to warn me that the road ahead may be dangerous but that I should still proceed. It alerts me, it keeps me on guard.

If you ask me, do I feel fear? I would say yes, I do feel fear, but in a different way to how others feel fear. How I would explain this is with an example. The usual form of fear is like a deer standing in the middle of the road completely frozen and unable to move while the oncoming car's high-beam lights get closer and closer. That is the sort of fear that I fear. If a situation occurs in my life where I am called upon to act in one way or another, I fear ever being like that deer, frozen, still, not acting. I fear ever being that way.

So, the only thing I fear is fear itself.

When the game is on the line and the clock is almost up, I am the one who wants the ball in my hand to take the winning shot. I would recommend for you to be this way. When you have a healthy self-esteem and you become a confident person, then when the storm gathers, you can be the one to step in and help. You can be the one to encourage and to support, the rock that others lean on. You won't fear being in that position, because you are unstoppable.

In 1941 Winston Churchill was asked to visit Harrow School and to give a speech before the students. In that speech he said to the students, "Never give in, never give in, never, never, never, never, in nothing great or small, large or petty. Never give in except to convictions of honour and good sense. Never yield to force, never yield to the overpowering might of the enemy."

Churchill was faced with a tremendous foe, but he did not let fear set in. I'm sure at times he didn't know what was going to happen next, but he did know that he was not going to give in. He would be persistent and determined to do whatever it took to defeat the enemy. He fought for justice and what was right, and he used fear in the right way.

No matter what challenges you face in your life, no matter what storm gathers on the horizon, whether it be a financial storm, a family storm, or that storm that can be the most destructive, the storm within yourself.

I say to you on this day that you should never give up and you should be determined, persistent. Use fear in the right way, as a warning of danger. At times, this will not be easy. You may feel that the weight of the whole world is on your shoulders.

If you feel this heavy weight on your shoulders, trust that you have the ability to conquer the worst of circumstances, that you have that rare ability to control your thoughts and that therefore you can control your actions.

Winston Churchill made a speech where he told the people of Britain that they would never give up, they would never surrender. They would fight the Germans on the beaches, they would fight them on the landing grounds, they would fight them in the mountains and in the streets, and they would never give up. By not giving up, they won the fight.

When life throws a hurricane at you, stand up and say to the storm, "I have the power to defeat you. Yes, you come to me with great force. You expect me to cower as many others have cowered before you. But you are wrong, my dear storm, I don't see your power, I just see your temporary existence. Yes, it is a powerful existence, but it is only temporary, whereas I am eternal. I have the power to stop you, so you can do no harm. You may be able to hurt my body, but you can never have dominion over my mind. My mind is my home, a home you cannot enter. I will use the power of my mind, my thoughts, to dissipate your strength and then I will see you cower away from me and dissipate before my very eyes and in that moment I will have been victorious because I am unstoppable."

When the storm comes into your life and you get knocked down, grab hold of something or someone and let it or them help you up. Gain your strength and gain control of your thoughts, and the storm will do you no harm.

Unfortunately, many people just let themselves be beaten down by the storm and they never try to get up.

Once upon a time, a man was walking past the circus and as he stopped to see what the circus was all about, he noticed there was a big powerful elephant standing near the tent with no attendant, no one controlling the massive beast.

The man saw that the elephant's leg had a thin chain around it. The chain around the elephant's leg was connected to a little stake that was wedged in the ground.

The man couldn't believe what he was seeing. If this

big strong animal wanted to be free, all he would have to do is to pull on the chain hard and it would come out of the ground instantly. Perplexed by this, he noticed an animal trainer a few hundred feet away, so he went over to speak with him.

He wanted to know why the trainer was not worried about the elephant getting away. The trainer said to him, "The reason why the elephant cannot escape is because of training." "Training?" replied the inquisitive man.

The trainer responded, "When the elephant was very young and small, we put the same chain around the same leg that he has on now as a full-grown adult elephant. We then drove a stake hard into the ground and set the stake in thick concrete. The little elephant would try and try to break free. He would try for weeks but the little fella did not have the strength to break free. After a number of weeks of trying to free himself, the little elephant just stopped trying."

"He believed that he could not ever be free. At that moment he was trained. So, as the elephant grew up into a big animal, all we had to do was put a small chain around one leg and just put a little stake in the ground. Whenever the big elephant moves and feels tension in the chain, he tells himself that he cannot get free and at that moment, he stops trying. He has convinced himself that he cannot be free and gives up. You see, he could be free, but he is chained in his mind."

Unfortunately, some people are this way. At one time, they tried at something and because they failed, they tell themselves that they can never succeed, thus training themselves for failure. All that big elephant needs to do is pull hard and he has the strength to bring that whole circus tent down. We are the same; we have the abilities to do amazing things, we have just been trained to think that we can't.

Don't be like the elephant. Don't convince yourself that you cannot do a certain thing. Be persistent, be determined.

Winston Churchill resolved in his heart that he would never quit, come what may. He would either be victorious or he would be dead in the street. He looked ahead and saw the possibilities. He had goals; he could see victory in sight. It would only be there if he never gave up.

Napoleon Hill tells a story about a man named Darby. Darby found some land where he thought there might be gold, so he got his pick and shovel and started digging. He dug with all his might with great excitement. While sweating from the hard work, he put his shovel into the ground and when it came out he discovered a shining piece of gold. Knowing that there might be a lot more gold in the ground and knowing that the pick and shovel would not be enough, he buried the site and went off to buy big machinery so he could dig deeper and see how far this vein of gold extended. He brought in the big machinery and started digging and the gold kept coming. He said to himself, "I could pay off all my debts with all this gold that I've discovered and then the real profits will flow in."

He kept digging and had more than enough to pay off his debts, but all of a sudden whilst digging, Darby noticed the vein of gold had dried up. There was no more to be found, so he dug a few more feet, but still no gold. He said to himself that this must be all that there is, and he quit.

He sold his machinery to a junk man while telling him of his find and his sudden misfortune. The junk man thought hard and decided to get a mining engineer to look at the site where Darby quit digging for gold. The engineer looked at the mine and realised immediately why the vein of gold had dried up. He said to the junk man, "Darby was not aware of faultlines." He explained, "When the earth moves, it can separate the vein of gold. Generally, it won't separate it too far, maybe only four or five feet. If you keep digging, you should pick up the vein of gold again." The junk man kept on digging and discovered millions of dollars' worth of gold. Darby had stopped three feet from gold.

I see people start a business and then they stick at if for a while, maybe six months or a year, but if they don't get the results that they expected, they just give up. They don't stick it out for any good length of time.

Sometimes for something to be successful, you need to stick at it for a long time. Some businesspeople I have heard about don't expect any profit from their business until a few years have passed. I am not saying that, no matter what happens, you have to continue down the road you have started on until it works. Sometimes you can plant your seeds year after year, but if the ground is contaminated, no matter how hard you try, you will never yield produce, so maybe you have to go and plant in another field.

It is your discretion about what to do that counts in business, but when it comes to you being unstoppable, persistence and never giving up is the thing that will make you successful.

Darby in our story just stopped when the gold vein dried up, but if he had been more persistent he would have kept digging and become a very rich man.

Persistence also does wonders for your mind. If you are persistent, then you will get results in your life because you are consciously aware that you have this quality. It gives you massive confidence to know that persistence is part of your character. In business, this quality can make you a very successful person.

If you are persistent in your relationships, in caring for your partner, your family, and your friends, you will be enriched by the experience.

Think of your mindset. If giving up is just not part of your makeup, then you will never give up on your goals until you reach them, you won't worry about problems in your life because you will know that no matter what comes up, you will persist until you find a solution. Knowing that you have the ability to persist will give you the confidence you need.

What if Sir Edmund Hilary hadn't possessed this quality of determination? The quality of persistence?

What about if he kept telling himself that he couldn't do it, that he was not good enough to climb Everest? Would he ever have reached the top?

As soon as the first big challenge came, he would have given up and if he didn't, then I'm sure he would have given up when the second one came along. When you want to reach the top of the highest mountain in the world, there will be life-threatening challenges along the way.

Many people didn't make it to the top of Everest, but the quality of persistence and determination helped Hilary and Tenzing reach the top, an amazing achievement.

How will developing the quality of persistence help you overcome some of your personal problems? What if you have a challenge with drugs, alcohol, smoking, or some other addiction? I am not a psychologist, but with an addiction we have engraved a pattern of thinking that is hard to break, with substance abuse we have fed our body and our brain on that substance so that now our body is constantly crying out for more, feeling like you will die if you do not continue with your addiction.

If we have trained our brain for so long in one direction, it will be very difficult to change overnight. But know that you can change. I completely disagree with one of the twelve steps of Alcoholics Anonymous, where you have to admit that you are powerless. This could not be further from the truth. You have tremendous power; you just have to start training your brain in a different direction.

Look over the section in this book that talks about

our thinking and our mind and learn to control your mind. One part of our brain is the moral part, the part where we have our values, and the other part is the survival part, the part that has no morals and is just for survival. This part can very strongly influence the part of the brain that reasons, the values part, but it cannot control it.

You are not powerless. If it is substance abuse, you have to swap a bad habit for a good habit and, yes, you may need to see someone and you may need to get support, but you do have power.

One way you can try to stop an addictive behaviour is with mindfulness. Be curious while you are involved in this addictive behaviour. Step out of your body, so to speak, and observe what is taking place. You know that this addictive behaviour is not good for you, but when you are mindful you internalise it and this might help you break free from it. If it is a sexual addiction, Napoleon Hill talks about sexual transmutation. Basically, since sexual desire is one of the most powerful forces in our body, you have to try and channel this energy, not to a sexual end but towards becoming successful. Channel it into your business, into your goals, your dreams. Put that energy to good use in other areas of your life.

With any addictive behaviour, you need to keep busy with life and never allow yourself to be bored. If it is a serious addiction, then please get help. But the best help is within you, to change your thinking from destructive to constructive, to give your brain something else to focus on rather than your bad habit.

Feel joy now. I can tell you from experience that when you can say that you are absolutely free from any addictions – except coffee, I'm taking that to the grave – you can live a life of bliss. Feel the feelings of there being nothing with a hold on you, being a prisoner of no one and no thing. That is true freedom. When you have full control of your thoughts, you can be the captain of your own ship and steer your life. Nothing will take control of you again.

To get to this stage, you will need the quality of persistence and determination. So, persist in your journey to accomplish your goals and have the confidence that no matter what barriers come up in your life, persistence and determination will pull you through.

SEVEN

In 1914, Sir Ernest Shackleton set out with his crew on the ship 'Endurance' and headed to the Antarctic. On their journey, Endurance became trapped in ice and, after some time, sank. This trapped Shackleton and his men on the floating ice. The men eventually made it to Elephant Island. Shackleton then took five men with him and set sail with a small boat and they spent sixteen days at sea to reach help. Eventually, they arrived at South Georgia Island, a journey of 1,300 km. The men then crossed the island to a whaling station. The remaining men of the Endurance were rescued in August 1916. Not one of Shackleton's men perished.

Sir Ernest Shackleton was a courageous man. Despite the dangers, he did what it took for his entire crew to survive, a true hero.

If Shackleton did not have the courage to cross the ocean to get help, all would have perished.

Many men in history have shown courage by giving their life so others can live. The saying goes that a courageous man dies once, whereas a coward dies a thousand times.

When a man is a coward, he dies internally over and over again.

Doing extremely difficult things for others, even though we don't benefit from it, is courageous. Being willing to take a hit for others is courageous.

A man was constantly depressed because his wife had cancer and eventually died. He went to see a psychiatrist and explained that he could not go on living without his wife. The doctor listened to the man and told him he had spared his wife a lot of pain. The man didn't understand what the doctor was saying, because his wife had passed away. The doctor explained that, by his wife dying before him, he had spared her the pain of seeing him suffering with an illness and dying slowly and then being in his current position, alone. The man had taken on that burden for his wife. She was no longer suffering. So, instead of thinking that he could not go on living, he should go on living so she could be spared the pain of losing him. The doctor explained that the man was sparing his wife the pain because she never lived with the loss of him. The man contemplated what the doctor had said and left his office with no need to ever return.

Sometimes it takes a lot of courage to continue when you have lost a loved one to death, especially if you have been with that person for many years. Sometimes your identity is tied up with that person and, now that they are gone, you have to rediscover who you are as an individual.

When someone I care about dies, I do mourn them but I very quickly turn that mourning into a celebration.

I celebrate the life that the person lived, even if only for a short while. I did this when my father died and to this day when I think of him a smile comes to my face because, in my mind, the life that he lived is worth celebrating and I can continue living my life with sweet memories.

There are other instances when courage is needed. When a family or a community is devastated by tragedy, I call upon you to be courageous, to be the rock, to be that strong person whom everybody can come to and lean on when life is tough. There were many people who were courageous in recent history, like Thomas Jefferson, Gandhi, Winston Churchill, Martin Luther King Jr., and Nelson Mandela. These people all stood up for what they believed in.

A remarkable act of courage occurred on 1st December 1955. A woman named Rosa Parks boarded a bus in Montgomery, Alabama and sat down. The bus driver asked Rosa Parks to relinquish her seat to a white man. You see, Rosa Parks was an African-American female and by law she had to give up her seat to a white person. Rosa Parks refused to give up her seat. It was an act of defiance, an act of courage against a racist society that treated African-American people as second-class human beings. Parks was arrested for her brave act of defiance. This led to the civil rights movement of the Montgomery Bus Boycott headed by Martin Luther King Jr. This civil rights movement continued and led to King giving his famous speech in Washington, known as the "I Have A Dream Speech."

Rosa Parks showed true courage. She had had enough of this kind of treatment and she wanted to take a stand against it.

Courage comes in many forms. Often it is an internal sense of doing what is right and just. Whether it is firefighters running into a burning building or a mother defending her child from a wild animal or just a random stranger giving his or her life to save someone else, we can all be courageous. I think we all have courage inside us, but many of us have not found it yet. One way to find that internal courageous spirit is to realise your self-worth and self-confidence. Lets now look at these qualities and see if you can find your worth, confidence, and courage.

EIGHT

Once upon a time in a faraway land, there was a farm boy. He was summoned by the Lord of his town. The Lord asked the farm boy to take one hundred pieces of gold to a castle far away. The farm boy asked the Lord, "Do I have soldiers coming with me to protect me from thieves?" The Lord, knowing that he had no one to spare but not wanting to frighten the boy, said, "No I don't have any guards to come with you, but don't be afraid, I have something even more powerful for you." At once the Lord took out a bright shining sword and continued, saying to the farm boy, "Take this with you. It is a special sword, it will protect you, it is the King's own personal sword, you will be safe, now go." The farm boy felt confident because he had the King's sword. Along his journey, the farm boy came across many thieves, some of them on their own and some in groups, but he always was victorious in protecting the gold. When the boy reached the castle, he delivered the gold and handed the King's sword back to the castle attendant. The farm boy said, "Here is the King's sword, it protected me on many occasions." At this, the attendant had a puzzled look on his face and said, "The King's sword?" "Yes," said the farm boy. The attendant continued, "Young man, the old King died many years ago and his heir is only seven years old, so this is not and never has been the King's sword." The farm boy left the castle perplexed. If that was not the King's sword, he thought, then it had no power, so it wasn't the sword that protected me, it was me, I was the one who defeated the thieves, I was the victorious one.

The farm boy finally realised that it was never the sword that gave him the ability to win the battles; all the sword did was give him the confidence to exhibit his own abilities. The farm boy didn't realise that he had worth, that he was confident. The farm boy had a giant living inside of him and all the sword did was encourage the giant to come out.

I say that we all have a giant resting inside of us, ready to come out. The day that changed my life forever was the day that I discovered my self-worth. When I discovered my worth, I started to soar. I realised that I had amazing abilities, not in an arrogant way but in a confident way, never assuming I am better than anyone but knowing that no matter what situation occurs in my life, I have the ability to deal with it.

I think you are the same. I am not sure where you are in your life, but I think I can help you find your self-worth and your confidence. One of the very first things that you can do, and need to do every day, is to sell you to you.

What person on this planet doesn't know what Coca-Cola is? Everyone knows Coke. So why does this company still advertise itself to the world? It is because they never want anyone, even for a brief moment, to forget who they are and the product they sell.

It's the same with you; you have to continue, on a daily basis, to sell you to you. You have to keep reminding yourself of all the good that you have done and are continuing to do.

There is no benefit in reliving in your mind the bad things that you've done. I mentioned in an earlier chapter that the mind is very powerful. When we make a mistake, we can learn from what we did so we never repeat the same mistake again, but to constantly relive in our minds the failures of our life will do us no good. Eradicate all negative thinking about what has happened in your past. Be in the present. You cannot do anything about the past, so if you keep dwelling on these events you will never build up your self-esteem and your confidence.

The only way to look into the past is to remember all the sweet moments of life, all the joy, the happiness, the bliss. Remember the times when you were successful, the times when you didn't fail, the times when you accomplished great things.

Many years ago, as a young man, my father left his home country of Italy and sailed the high seas to Australia. I am sure he didn't know how he was going to get by in Australia. He didn't speak the language, he didn't know what he was going to do for work or where he was going to live, but he did it anyway and that took courage and confidence. In his later years, I'm not sure if he ever reflected on that accomplishment, but he should have. Those are the kinds of memories we should reflect on to give us confidence today. Remember the big things you did and, more importantly, how you overcame the challenges.

Many battles in courtrooms today are fought over precedents that were set years ago. If someone is on trial, the lawyers will look back through the records and see where someone has been through the same ordeal and won their court battle, and then they use that case as a precedent for their current trial.

Do the same with your past, look for precedents that you have set many years ago. If you overcame something back then, you can overcome it now and this will give you confidence today.

So, only dwell on the past if it will lift you up; if it is negative in any way, don't let it come into your mind, fight the thought with that soldier who stands at the door to your mind. Even a little negative thought can be dangerous.

If your friend gives you a glass of water that has poison in it, you will die. If you enemy gives you a glass of water that has poison in it, again, you will die. So, whether it is a friend or an enemy, if you drink the water, you will die. It doesn't matter how you get the poison or where it comes from, the effect is the same. So, whether about the past, the present, or the future, if you take in the poisonous substance of negative thinking, you will be affected.

What about the present moment? How do we build our self-esteem?

First, let's look at external forces, meaning the people in our lives. These people can have a major impact on our life. Whether it is friends or family members, you need to resolve that you will let no one bring you down or talk to you as if you have no worth. From this moment on, you will only spend time with people who see your worth and are not trying to tear you down.

The stories I have heard of family members who treat one another like garbage are astonishing. So, I say this now, if you have a friend or a family member who is making you feel worthless on purpose, then please walk away. They say that blood is thicker than water. Well, blood makes up around seven percent of our body whereas water is about sixty percent. I am not saying for you to do this lightly, it should be done with tears, but you cannot live your life when someone who is supposed to be in a position of trust is intentionally making you feel worthless. If you stay in that relationship you will never find self-worth, it will become lost forever. You wouldn't stay in a relationship with someone who physically abuses you, so why would you stay in a relationship with someone who verbally abuses you. The putdowns might not be severe, but remember that even just a little poison can have an effect on you. If it doesn't kill you the first day, then a little poison everyday will eventually do it.

Spend time with people who will lift you up, ones who will encourage you to follow your dreams. Ones who won't say that you're not good enough to do what you set out to do. These ones will say to you that you can do it, that you are a special person who has great abilities and great potential, and that you can be, do, or have anything you want. The ones who treat you like this every day, these are the ones you should spend time with. That's how life should be.

When I removed all the negative people from my life, my life soared; no one was holding me back anymore. I didn't do it lightly, but it had to be done. The chains that held me back were broken and I was free. Now the only person who could stand in my way was me.

Let's talk about you now. You are the only one who can stand in your way. Your self-talk is so important. How do you speak to yourself? It all starts when that sun rises in the morning. When you get up and out of bed and look in the mirror, what do you say to yourself? At that moment in the morning, what you tell yourself will affect the rest of your day until that sun goes down. You can either look in the mirror and say that you have no worth or you can look in the mirror and say to yourself that you are beautiful, you have so much potential, you can accomplish amazing things, and you will treat people in an amazing way. You can say that you will smile throughout the day and you will enrich people's lives, that you are willing at any time to come to the rescue of the downtrodden. That you will make people feel better about themselves because you feel great about yourself. That who you are on the inside is beautiful and you are going to show the world that beauty and that when a problem shows up, you have the ability to handle it because you realise that you are an amazing person created in an amazing way to do amazing things, to overcome any obstacle, and that the universe is on your side helping you to be great.

If you tell this to yourself in the morning, every morning, how will your day be? Once you tell yourself this, think of how much better your day will be if you start to think about all the great things in your life. Spend ten minutes in the morning while you are having breakfast and be grateful for all the good in your life. Gratitude plays an amazing part in our lives. See yourself as Superman. There is a big **S** on your chest. What could this world challenge you with that you couldn't handle? Remember that you are pure energy and you attract into your life what you think about. When you start the day off like this, you will constantly attract good things into your life during the day. If you are confronted with a negative person, then just walk away, protect self-worth, protect happiness.

At times things won't go your way, but never fear failure. Failure is a term I give no meaning to anymore. When things don't go according to plan, then that's OK, learn from it and take a new direction.

If there is something that you are not confident about doing, then I say you should go ahead and do it until you become confident. If you are not confident to travel on your own, then go travelling on your own and know that you will become confident at it. If you are scared to fail, then just fail at something. Start a business that you know you will fail at and watch it as it goes under and then you will know how it feels and you will become more confident when you start another business. I say this in a humorous way of course, but I think everybody should go bankrupt before they're thirty, so they know how it feels and still have plenty of time to get themselves going again.

My point in saying this is to encourage you to gain the confidence you need and the experience you need. So, live life to the fullest and never be afraid of what may come.

I spoke about the past and about what we can say to ourselves today, but what about gaining self-esteem and confidence going into the future?

I truly believe that the future has not been written yet. I don't believe in destiny. I believe we create our future, we create our destiny. So, don't worry about what may or may not happen. That just saps the joy from today. The only thing we should think about in the future is all the good things that we are going to create, the dreams, the goals, the success. These are the things that I encourage you to think about on a daily basis. Don't think about the what-ifs. You know these, what if this happens and what if that happens? If we think about the what-ifs, then we are bringing those things into existence. Know that, whatever comes, you have the ability to handle it and it will all be OK. If there is a challenge, then you have the ability to grow and meet the challenge.

Start small and become confident in little things and then you can grow and become confident in bigger things. It's like when you want to grow a muscle, you start exercising with a light weight and then move up to a heavier weight and, when the muscle is strained the most, that's when it will grow. If you are trying to grow your biceps, the repetition that will make it grow is not the first one. It is the final repetition that makes all the difference. The hardest repetition is the last one and then the muscle grows. Your confidence will grow when you are faced with trials, but if you are aware that the purpose of trials is to help you grow, then that will give you confidence to push through.

Once upon a time, a boy was walking home from school. As he was nearing his home, a big dog came running around the corner barking and growling and started chasing him. The boy started running with all his might and just made it into his front yard before the dog reached him. The next day on his way home the dog appeared again and started chasing the boy. The boy ran and safely made it into his yard. This happened for the next two days. On the fifth day, the dog came out barking right on schedule and instead of running away, the boy picked up a thick stick and faced the angry dog. As the dog was approaching, the boy was ready to swing, but when the dog was two metres from the boy, he noticed that the dog had no teeth. The boy just yelled at the dog and it ran away.

Most problems in life which give us a lack of

confidence and low self-esteem have no teeth. They are just all bark and no bite. Sometimes, we are limited by our own belief that the problem has teeth, when often it doesn't.

The word confidence comes from the Latin *confidere*, which means to have full trust. You can have full trust in yourself. If you cannot trust yourself, then whom can you trust? if not you, then who? If not now, then when? This is the time, today, to start looking at yourself differently. You have power and if you have the will, you will find the way. Each and every day, act confidently and act as if you have high self-esteem. Go out into the world and see these qualities in other people.

Trust people. Unfortunately, we live in a world of distrust. Many years ago, it was 'Trust someone until they prove that they cannot be trusted.' Today, it's 'Don't trust anyone until they prove they can be trusted.'

Don't be like this. Society has changed for the worse. Don't be like everyone else. Trust from the get-go, until people show that they can't be trusted. I am not saying to be gullible, so use your discretion. If you meet someone for the first time, trust them. If you greet someone with a genuine smile and a handshake and do not trust them, you are being false to yourself. Mistrust will have an effect on you without you even realising it.

Trust people and they will trust you, build people's self-esteem up and it will build yours up. Encourage people to be confident and you will be confident. Smile all day, knowing that the past has no hold on you anymore and you have once and for all broken the chains that kept you bound. In all your dealings, love more, give more, and smile more. Be assured that you can handle any situation that arises and that you are worth so much.

When the sun goes down and you fall asleep, the universe paints a picture of your day and, in the evening, the little birds fly in and take out the painting. As the birds are flying the painting away to a secure location, one bird will turn to the other and say, "Check out the painting of his day today. Wow, a masterpiece."

NINE

There was a Swiss man named William Tell who was a marksman with the crossbow. He lived in the mountains with his son and one day he came down into the village and saw a pole in the main square with a hat on top of it.

People were gathering around the pole bowing down to it. The pole was erected by Duke Gressler and it was his hat that was on top of the pole. Gressler hated Tell and when he noticed that Tell was not bowing down to the pole, he became furious. He arrested Tell and gave him an ultimatum. Gressler tied Tell's boy to the pole and put an apple on his head. Tell was ordered to shoot the apple off his son's head or they would put his son to death before his very eyes.

What would Tell do? Although he was an expert marksman, he was worried that the boy might move slightly and that he would shoot his own son. But he had no choice. He put one arrow in his quiver and another arrow in his crossbow, aimed for the apple, and shot the arrow. The arrow split the apple in two. Noticing the second arrow in his quiver, the Duke asked Tell why he had another arrow in his quiver. Tell told the Duke that if he had hurt his boy with the first shot, the second arrow was for the Duke. Furious at what Tell said, he had Tell arrested and sent to the dungeons for life.

On the way to the prison, a storm hit the lake and the boat captain asked the Duke if Tell could be freed from his chains so he could help steer the boat to safety. The Duke agreed and Tell steered the boat to shore. Once they hit the shore, Tell fled and the Duke pursued him. Seeing the Duke coming, Tell leapt out of the bushes and killed him. Thus came an end to the tyrant Duke Gessler.

This was a tale I heard when I was in Switzerland. Tell was a symbol for the Swiss people against the aggression of the Hapsburg emperors.

When I travel, I travel to learn. I want to learn about the cultures I come into contact with. I like to add travel into all my writings because we can learn so much from other cultures to help us become better people.

When you travel to a different country, there is always a theme to it. Every country has its story, its own legends. They are usually stories of a man or group of people who rise up against tyranny and save the common people. For the most part, I would say that these tales are true. Some are legends with some truth to them, but embellished over time. This kind of hero stands out as a symbol of freedom.

The Scottish people have William Wallace, who stood up against the English army and was martyred while trying to help them gain their freedom from their English overlords.

Then you have Robin Hood, who with his men lived

in Sherwood Forest and was a hero to the people because he robbed the rich and gave to the poor. There is a lot of speculation about Robin Hood. Was he a hero? Was he a criminal? Was there even a man named Robin Hood? Scholars have found a few references to a man called Robert Hood and some people think there were many men called Robert Hood. They think there was one original Robert Hood who was a villain and robbed people and that the nickname Robert Hood was given to many thieves. There were ballads sung by minstrels that spoke of this man. Whatever the local legend is, people want to believe that it was a tale of Good vs Evil.

Then there was King Arthur and his supposed birthplace of Tintagel, England, a place where lovers of the legend of Arthur gather to try and learn more about this man who was a hero of the people for fighting the Saxons.

While fighting his son Mordred, Arthur's sword Excalibur was thrown into the lake and never found. People still search that lake for Excalibur! Arthur has become one of those legends, told from generation to generation. Was he real or was he just a legend? Travelling to these historic sites really excites me. They say that history is written by the victors, so you may never find the real truth of these legends, but the mystery is exciting.

Then you can go from mystery to established historical facts. One of my favourite moments was looking directly at the Colosseum in Rome for the first time. Near the Colosseum is the Arch of Constantine. Roman Emperors and generals passed under this triumphal arch on their return to Rome.

While standing there, you can picture the people cheering the Emperor on as his chariot circled the Colosseum and then entered the Roman Forum. You can let your imagination run wild in this location, picturing Emperor Nero performing a play and figures like Julius Caesar, Vespasian, and many others. What would life have been like at that time? When you research the history, you can sit on a big rock in the Roman Forum and just use your imagination and make it all come to life in your mind.

You can leave the Forum and walk a few minutes and you will enter a field that has an oval gravel track, the gravel track of the Circus Maximus. This is where chariot races were held. You can hear the cheers and feel the ground rumble as the horses gallop past with great power, directed by furious chariot drivers.

Making history come alive is one of the best things about travel. I say to people they should learn about the legends and learn about the facts of the places they travel to.

I love London, not the modern city but the old city in amongst the modern city. People say that London is just another city, but when I travel there I don't see modern, I block out all that's modern, my imagination takes over and I am transported back hundreds of years into the past. I see the knights riding on their horses with their swords by their side. I see the merchants, the peasants, and I even imagine the variety of smells. Pretend you are walking through a 12th century marketplace, starting in the forest, walking into a small town, and picture what it would have been like nine hundred years ago. This is what makes travel exciting.

The other part of travel that I love is learning about other cultures that can enrich my life. In my last book, I spoke about my travels and I will talk a little more about them now. From West to East or North to South, although human beings are all basically the same, their cultures can be completely different.

My time in Argentina was a remarkable experience. In Argentina, the warmth and friendliness between people is on another level. When you get to know them, you find a kind and courteous people, people who are trusting and warm. They are a generous people and I was treated kindly by everyone I met. I am sure they have unkind people as well, but it was an overall positive feeling that touched me.

The Argentines taught me to look for the best in everyone I met, to be warmer, friendlier, and kinder and to help out people who need help whom I don't even know and to do this with a willing and cheerful heart.

Barcelona was another place that I truly loved, because even though Barcelona is a part of Spain, it is proudly in a region of its own, Catalonia. The Catalan language is spoken and some of the people of Barcelona want to become independent of Spain. The people of Barcelona are a passionate lot with a real zest and passion for life. They laugh, they love, and they cry. They are a people who know who they are and what their culture is all about.

In my travels I learnt many things about the people

of Barcelona. They seem to cherish each day they live and they live life to the fullest. I guess you don't know what tomorrow brings, so what a nice way to live.

Travel has enriched my life and I encourage you to travel more. It saddens me when I hear of places like the US, where most people only get two weeks a year for a vacation. How can you possibly enrich your lives with other cultures if you have no time to meet and discover these cultures.

I can tell you the best places to visit in the world, but let's just say you have two to three weeks for a vacation. I will give you a good vacation plan. It gives you a couple of cultures to see and a mix of city and surf.

Fly into Milan, Italy. Spend one day there and no more, there are a few things to see in Milan, but one day is enough.

Get the train and go up to Lake Como. Hire a boat for half a day or even a day and spend that time on the lake, eating nice food and drinking nice wine.

After Como, if you want a short trip on the side you can visit Venice, a city on water. The Venetians fled the mainland and built homes out in the swamps in hopes that the barbarians would not come there and attack them. Now, it's a major city with lots of stairs and bridges, so pack light. In Venice you will learn all about a city that was once a powerhouse of commerce, a city feared for its ability to build a warship in only a few days. Venice is the most romantic city I have visited. Take a ride on a gondola with someone you love.

After Venice, via a few different transport options, make your way down to Rome. If you choose to drive or train it, you can head through Tuscany and visit some nice little towns and a vineyard or two. When you reach Rome, bathe in more than two thousand years of history. Stay out until late, walk the cobbled stones eating a gelato, stroll along the beautiful streets.

After Rome, head up to Florence, the home of the Renaissance. Hear names like Michelangelo and Leonardo da Vinci being whispered in the streets. These creative men created works of art for the leaders of the time, like the Medici family and the Popes. Discover the city where modern humanism was born.

After Florence, head towards the coast and stop off for an hour at Pisa to get a shot of that famous leaning tower. After Pisa, jump on a train and hop on and off the train at any point you like along the Italian and French Riviera.

Spend a day or two in the Cinque Terra. My favourite hillside town in the Cinque Terra is Vernazza, but you should visit all five towns. See how the simple life is lived. The views are amazing.

Along the Italian Riviera, you can stop off at Portofino or Sanremo.

After these beautiful stops, you will arrive in Monaco. You have to spend time in Monte Carlo, but maybe sleep in a nearby town because the accommodation is very expensive, especially in Grand Prix week, when I was there last time.

Keep heading up the French Riviera and spend a day or two in Nice, walk the boardwalk, drink French wine, and sunbathe on a rocky beach next to beautiful blue waters.

Pass through Cannes and pay a lot of money for a salad! Walk the streets with multimillionaires and marvel at the wealth on display.

Head to Saint Tropez and just indulge in food and drink and relax spending time where the big movie stars go to relax. After Saint Tropez, go back to Nice and catch a plane or train to Paris.

Finish your holiday in this city. Learn about the French Revolution and go out to the Palace of Versailles to see the gardens. Learn about the final days of the Knights Templar organisation, drink coffee, and eat croissants. Then it's time to go home. Throughout this trip there are lots of things to do in the towns you visit and lots of great little side trips.

On this trip, you will learn about the non-stop, no-nonsense banking, finance, and industrial area of North Italy. Learn about the Romans, past and present. People who live in Rome don't see themselves as Italians, but as Romans. You will see a lot of seaside towns and you will get a feel of their quiet and slow life. You will see where the rich holiday and live and you can picture yourself being there one day if you want. You finish with the amazing history of Paris.

When you travel, keep an open mind and never judge a culture until you have really immersed yourself in it. Learn from the locals. Don't just go to the tourist parts but also get off the beaten path and go to where local people hang out, where you will see the real culture. Make friends, be a local.

Travel will test you. It will test your patience, especially dealing with people at airports and bus and train terminals, but it will be OK because after reading this book, you will know how to completely control your mind, your thoughts, and your actions.

Be inquisitive as you travel, try foods that you wouldn't normally try, and drink drinks you normally don't drink. In Greece, drink *ouzo*, in Italy, drink *grappa*. When in England, have some tea. Be a cultural chameleon and blend into your surroundings. More importantly, be open to learning new things that will make you a better person and that you can bring back home with you so you not only enrich yourself, but also your family and your community.

If you don't have the finances to travel, then apply the things I have mentioned in this book and set as a goal the money you will need to travel. Never begrudge the money spent on travel, because you could never buy this education at a university, no matter how many history classes you took or how many books you read.

Through travelling you will gain confidence and your self-esteem will rise. You will see that you are capable of surviving and thriving in places far from home.

Today you can do things that even kings in times past could not do because of distance and danger. It was impossible for them to go around the world even with their armies, though the Romans sure tried! You have this gift, keep that firmly in mind. Travel will enrich your soul. It will help you discover who you are and motivate achieving your purpose in life, whatever that may be.

TEN

Colonel Sanders was 65 years old and he was broke. He had his first social security cheque of $105 in one hand and a killer chicken recipe in the other. He lived in his car for two years trying to sell that chicken recipe to restaurant owners.

He was rejected 1,009 times before a restaurant owner was willing to use his recipe. He heard one thousand "No's" before he heard a "Yes", but he never gave up on his dream. He learnt from each failure and now the story of Kentucky Fried Chicken is in the history books. How many "No's" would you have put up with, before you would quit on a dream?

Failure is a part of life. For some reason, many people are terrified by this thing we call failure. Children, for some reason, are not. When a baby tries for the first time to get up and walk, after he falls down four or five times, does the baby say to himself, "Ah well, I gave this walking thing a try, it seems it won't work for me. I might as well just crawl on the ground for the next 70 or 80 years." That's absurd. That baby will keep trying to walk until he walks. Ahh, that magic word, "until." No matter what we are trying to achieve in life, we need to keep trying until we achieve it. Failure is just a part of the process.

Failing does not mean that we are unintelligent, it does not mean we are not wise, nor that we are not good enough or have no worth. Some people act as if this is the case when they fail at something. They feel so bad about what has happened that they give up and never try again. I have a game for you: cast your mind back through history and see how many things would have never happened if people had given up after the first failure or two.

In our development from tribes to empires to global economy, the world would be a very different place if people had given up after the first one or two unsuccessful attempts.

This is what matters; not that you failed, but whether you continue after you have failed. Many people today start a business and when they fail, they just give up, they don't fight. If they lose the business, they just stop. That is the worst kind of failure. That failure will give you no confidence and you will never muster the courage to start again. In a boxing match, when a fighter is knocked to the ground, the referee gives him a count of ten seconds to get up. If he doesn't get up in those ten seconds, the fight is over and he has lost.

Sometimes in life, when a storm hits, you get a ten-second count, so to speak, and if you want to stay in the fight, you need to get up as quickly as possible and keep fighting. Never give up and never surrender.

Can we learn anything from the failures of others?

Do we need to fail to learn?

This chapter is dedicated to those who have completely failed in life.

Me personally, I don't mind failing because I eventually come to a realisation of another way to do something. If it doesn't work and I keep failing, I will eventually work it out.

When Thomas Edison was asked about his many failed attempts on the road to creating the incandescent light bulb, he said he didn't fail, he just tried many times and thus found out many ways it wouldn't work. He said that he only needed to make it work one time, and that he eventually did.

Little failures are fine, but what we don't want is to make massive mistakes on an ongoing basis, because that can lead us on a downward spiral with no return.

Learning from someone's failures can help us not to fail. There are many people in history who are great examples of what not to do. If these people could come and give a seminar today, I would be in the front row listening and taking notes about what not to do.

So, for a moment, let's please invite these men onto the stage and hear their stories.

The first person in today's seminar is the historical man Judas Iscariot. If a name was ever aligned with betrayal and failure, it is the name Judas.

Judas started with a small desire that got out of control, which led to his downfall.

Judas started off as a money collector for his master

and was slowly stealing money out of the moneybox. This led to a greed that would soon get out of hand. He loved money so much that, in the end, his greed made him betray his master for thirty pieces of silver and turn him over to people who wanted to kill him.

That was a sizeable amount back in the day he lived in, but look what greed for money led this man to do. He betrayed his master with a kiss. His master was turned over to his enemies and he was put to death. Judas the traitor sold out his master for pure greed.

After his master was put to death, Judas was so ashamed of what he had done that he tried to give the money back, as if that would make any difference. The men he had betrayed his master to would not take the money back, so Judas threw the money on the ground and went out and hanged himself.

What do you think Judas is telling the audience in the seminar today, what do you think he would say?

He would say that greed and the love of money can destroy you, if you let it. He would say not to sacrifice your values by just going after money. Money is great for what it can buy and the lifestyle it can bring, but if you give up the world for it, what would you have left?

So, on your journey to becoming successful and unstoppable, don't sacrifice your family, friends, or values by just going after your dreams. Be alert to the desire for money. That desire is fine as long as it doesn't turn you into a monster. You would never want to become like the traitor Judas and go just for money at the expense of everyone else, because if you do, in the end, it won't make you happy. It led Judas to take his own life.

The example of Judas is a major one and I'm sure that you wouldn't go as far as him in trying to make your dreams and goals come true, but always keep in mind that failures can be good but a failure of that magnitude can never be good, and we should learn from that.

If I was to ask you, what name is synonymous with Evil, what name would come to your mind?

Yep, you guessed it, Adolf Hitler, he is the next presenter in our seminar.

I don't want to talk a lot about this man; he doesn't deserve his name being mentioned. But if there was one man who was a complete failure, a man who was truly evil and had many people under him, whom he fed his evil thoughts to, it was Hitler.

I don't know where it all went wrong for this man. I don't know if he was burning little dolls as a child, but somewhere along the line he lost any sense of empathy or humanity. He lost any sense of what is right and decent. If the devil wanted to come and materialise in a man's form, then it would be the form of Adolf Hitler. The warning here is to watch and guard your thoughts from an early age.

If we start having bad thoughts towards a person, or towards a race of people, then that is the time to put a stop to it immediately. The thing with negative thoughts is that they can build on each other and get hotter and hotter until one day they explode.

One day, the thoughts of Hitler got so bad that they exploded, and he was in a position to do major harm.

The world didn't know about the horrors of the concentration camps until the war was over and Allied forces had invaded Germany and Poland.

I am sure if the Allied forces had known what this evil man was doing behind his borders, they would have conquered the Germans a lot sooner. It is amazing what human suffering and empathy can motivate a nation to do. The world would have stormed those camps.

Human life had no meaning to this man. In his book *Man's Search for Meaning*, Victor Frankl tells of his arrival at one of the German concentration camps.

The prisoners were all stripped of all their possessions and lined up in a row. They were required to walk past a senior SS guard for inspection. The guard had one arm across his body and the other arm sticking up resting on the other arm. He had one finger pointing up. When a prisoner approached the guard, the guard would either gesture with the one finger left or right. Little did the prisoners realise that this little gesture of his finger assigned them their fate. Signalling with his finger in one direction meant life in the camp, signalling in the other direction meant death in the gas chambers.

To decide in such a manner from person to person, who will live and who will die is despicably evil.

During Hitler's presentation in the seminar, I would learn from what he did. I would never start down a road that he started down. I would never let my empathy for other humans slowly fade. I would see each human being as a special creation. If I started feeling negative towards another human being, I would remind myself not to even take the first step toward evil and I would destroy any negative thoughts that I had for that other human being.

The name Adolf Hitler should be deleted from this world. The only good thing about remembering that name is remembering what happened, so we never let anything like it happen again.

We have had two speakers in our seminar thus far, the traitor Judas Iscariot and the evil Adolf Hitler.

Let's see who our third speaker is.

Walking onto the stage is Maximilien Robespierre.

Maximilien Robespierre was a French lawyer who became tired of the way King Louis XVI was running France. He was the man who spearheaded the beginning of the French Revolution. He wanted Liberty, Equality, and Fraternity.

The French people were starving while Queen Marie Antoinette was spending their money without a care in the world. Her fancy clothes were elaborate, her homes palatial. It's OK for a King and Queen to have the things they want, but not while their subjects are starving.

I am not going to say one way or the other if the revolution was a good thing or a bad thing for France. French people have many different views on the matter, but it would have been much better if they could just have replaced the King with one who cared about the condition of the people.

This part of today's seminar is about how the man Robespierre changed in the process. At the beginning of the revolution, he wanted freedom and equality for all. He realised he would need to put some people to death to improve things for the French people.

To do this in what he thought would be the most humane way to put someone to death, he used the guillotine. It was said at that time that the guillotine was the most humane way to put someone to death because of how quick it was.

After the King and Queen met their end by this device, Robespierre became a different person. He had gained power, but he was frightened that he would lose that power and that the people might revert back to the monarchy, so he condemned many people to death without even a trial, one after another. It was said that, at the height of the revolution, they guillotined up to a thousand people a month.

If you were heard saying anything bad about the new government, you were put to death. Rumour had it that if you didn't talk enthusiastically about the new government, you would face the guillotine.

Power, fear, and paranoia set in for Robespierre. Each week he would have a list of people to be executed. This man had strayed far from his earlier days when he wanted equality for the people. He became a dictator. One fateful day he made a big mistake.

He told the National Assembly that he had another list of people to face the guillotine. But his big mistake was that he didn't inform the Assembly of the names on the list, so the Assembly members thought that their names might be on the list for execution. So, before Robespierre had a chance to reveal the list, the Assembly had him arrested and sent him to the guillotine. He was executed on the same device where he had sent so many people.

The lesson I got out of Maximilien Robespierre's seminar talk was to always evaluate yourself throughout life.

Ask yourself, is my view on life starting to change? Are my morals and my sense of justice becoming weaker? If I end up in some position of power, how would I act?

The saying goes that power corrupts and absolute power corrupts absolutely. Power or responsibility can be hard to manage.

If we are in a position of responsibility, whether it is in our family or our company or our city or our country, how do we go about wielding our power? Robespierre started off with good intentions, but he let fear and paranoia set in, to the point where he started to lose his empathy for people and created a bloodbath instead.

So, monitor your actions and your feelings. When you want to do good for people, always do good with a pure and right motive.

Today's seminar is almost concluded, but there is one more speaker left. All of a sudden, while sitting in the audience, I hear a loud shout of "Sic semper tyrannis" ('Thus always to tyrants').

Yes, the voice is coming from John Wilkes Booth, the man who shot President of the United States Abraham Lincoln.

The American Civil War had just come to an end. The South, which believed it was a man's right to own another human being as a slave, had been defeated. The North, led by President Lincoln, thought that no man should ever own another man and was determined to abolish slavery.

Lincoln thought that, since he would never be anybody's slave, he should never have a slave. His course was right and it was just. It was correct that no man should own another man.

In time, slavery was abolished permanently in the United States. But on that fateful night, five days after the war had ended with the South's surrender, Lincoln and his wife attended the theatre. The President's guard left his side for a brief moment and that was when Booth chose his time to strike. He entered the President's box and shot him, shouting "Sic Semper Tyrannis" as he jumped down to escape.

Booth was a Southern white supremacist and he was caught, tried, and executed soon after the assassination. Unfortunately, there are small groups of people today who still have a white supremacist mentality and see other human beings as being beneath them.

The lesson I received in this part of our seminar was to remove any sort of hatred from our heart. If we feel that we have a negative attitude towards someone of a different race, acknowledge it and then do something about it. One thing that I have learnt from travelling and seeing many different cultures is that we may seem different, but in the end we are all the same.

Lincoln was trying to better his people and himself, to elevate the thinking of the United States to a new level of humanity. I find when people try to do good things and better themselves, there are always a few who try to tear them down.

Once upon a time, there was a King who was absent from his people in a faraway place. One of the King's officials sent a messenger to tell the king what was happening in his city, where some men were becoming very wealthy and successful in his absence.

A messenger was sent to relay this message to the King. After many weeks of travelling, the messenger met up with the King in a wheat field. As they walked in the wheat field, the messenger relayed what was going on in the King's domain. While the messenger was talking, the King was grabbing heads of grain, cutting them off, and leaving them on the ground to be trampled, without saying a word. The King kept doing this over and over again.

After the messenger had finished relaying his message, he returned to the King's land. Upon arrival, the King's official asked the messenger what the King's reply was. The messenger relayed what had happened and how he was talking to the King and how the King just kept chopping off heads of grain, which was strange because it was the best part of the crop. The messenger was perplexed because the King had not said anything, but the official was not perplexed. He knew exactly what the King meant without the King saying even one word. He dismissed the messenger, called in the King's General, and ordered him to round up all the men who had become extremely wealthy in the King's absence and put them all in prison for the rest of their lives.

In Australia, we don't put people to death for becoming wealthy or successful or for bettering themselves through personal development. But we do use a phrase a lot, that phrase being "Tall Poppy Syndrome." Anyone who gets too big, or does too well, or achieves a lot, people want them cut down just like the heads of grain the King cut off.

People want you to do well, just not that well. It's sad, because we should all be cheering one another on. Men hated Lincoln because he was trying to do what was right, whether they agreed with it or not.

Booth thought Lincoln was an evil person for trying to abolish slavery.

Never think someone is selfish because they are trying to improve their life. As you read this book and apply what you read, be careful whom you tell and whom you share it with. As you become a successful, happy, unstoppable person, only tell people who will encourage you to continue, not the ones who will try and cut you down. Your success just reminds those people of their lack of success.

The seminar has concluded. Judas Iscariot, Adolf Hitler, Maximilien Robespierre, and John Wilkes Booth have left the stage. What a lesson of what not to do or become.

You may say, 'I would never become like these men', and I'm sure you're right, especially because you invested in this book. But I would look at any percentage of similarity. If you ask me how much I want to be like Hitler, I would say not even one percent. I would find out what books Hitler read and I wouldn't read them. I would find out what music he listened to and I wouldn't listen to it. I would find out what coffee shop he went to for his morning coffee and I would never go there.

But, unfortunately, there are people who are similar in many ways to Hitler and have a high percentage of him in them. So, if there is any percentage of these men in us, we need to stomp on it as soon as possible. Betrayal, evil, lack of empathy, unrestrained power, racism, or jealousy are qualities we don't want in us even to a small degree.

Learn from other people's mistakes and try not to go down the path they went down. If you know someone who has failed all their life, I would suggest you take that person out for dinner and afterwards write down all the things that made him or her fail and do none of those things. Be sure you pick up the bill for the meal!

So, I hope that you can see that failure can be a good thing or a bad thing. Little failures can make us into a good person, but massive failures of values and beliefs can never be a good thing. You will find that soon you won't call these little failures, failures anymore because if you keep trying you have never failed.

In your journey to become unstoppable, stick to your values. Live by them, let them help you on your journey. Look to people who have achieved good things, study these people and learn from them. We need to see up ahead on life's road and see what could come up and protect ourselves against it now. Do this and never give up on doing what is good.

CONCLUSION

Once upon a time a grandfather was teaching life lessons to his grandson. He said to the boy, "There is a fight that goes on in all men, between two wolves.

One wolf is anger, greed, pride, arrogance, fear, worry, superiority, self-pity, and resentment.

The other wolf is love, joy, peace, bliss, happiness, hope, trust, and kindness.

These two wolves are battling very hard with each other."

The grandson asked his grandfather, "Which wolf will win?"

The grandfather responded, "The one you feed."

Unfortunately, we are all imperfect. We have a side of us that can lead us to ruin if we let it. The only difference is, which side do we feed? Which one do we focus on, entertain, and live from day to day? That one will show up in our life.

Remember what we spoke about in this book, that thoughts are things. You will become whatever you think about, whichever thought you feed. If you go about your day thinking that the universe is against you and that life is tough, then it will be that way.

If you go through the day thinking that the universe is on your side and life is easy, you will experience that reality. Yes, some tough times may come your way, but it is your thinking, your attitude, that will make all the difference.

What are the worst things a human can experience?

I would say that living life in a Nazi concentration camp has to be right up there. So, if a man like Viktor Frankl can go through that experience and realise that he had control over his thinking and his feelings, then we can do the same with the challenges in our life.

Frankl said in an interview, "Ultimate freedom remains always available to ourselves. That is the freedom to take a stand to whatever conditions may confront us. How we react to the unchangeable conditions is up to ourselves. In other words, if we cannot change the situation, we always have the last freedom to change our attitude to that situation."

This is the last human freedom.

Trust that you have the ability to control your thoughts, your feelings, and your actions. No one can take this away from you.

At times you may think that you can't do this, but please trust me when I say that you can.

You are a special creation, endowed with amazing creative abilities. Start with small things and work up to big things.

Put little stickers around your office, your car, and your house.

On these stickers write the words "Feeling" and "Thinking".

Throughout the day, look at them and remind yourself to always monitor these things. If you are not sure about what you are thinking, how you are feeling will tell you. If you are not sure what you are feeling, your thoughts will tell you.

In time you won't need the stickers and this monitoring will just happen naturally. When I first started, I had the stickers for about two months before I didn't need to remind myself anymore, and now I just monitor these things naturally.

It's nice to read about how you can completely change your life, but it takes action. You have to start putting into practice the things I have talked about in this book.

The saying goes that to know and not to do, is not to know.

So, do take action, start somewhere.

You will be amazed at the changes that will occur when you eliminate anything negative from your thoughts and your life and just focus on the positive things.

When I play golf and I make my tee shot, if I hit the ball just a few millimetres to one or other side, it means that either the ball will land on the fairway or it will go out of bounds off a massive slice.

Likewise, with just a little change you will see a big difference in your life.

You won't be able to stand hearing negative things anymore and you won't be able to stay near negative people for long. Just their vibe will make you want to run in the other direction. You will find it unnatural to entertain bad thoughts.

Just start with one day, or even with just one hour. A successful hour leads to a successful day. A successful day leads to a successful week. A successful week leads to a successful month. A successful month leads to a successful year. A successful year leads to a successful life.

One step, one millimetre.

Whatever your goals in life are, give them massive value. If you want money, then give the world massive value and you will have all the money you need.

If it is a loving relationship you want, give massive value to qualities that will attract and keep a loving person in your life. Be the person that you are trying to attract. If you want a loving person, then give love. If you want a generous person, then be generous. If you want money, give money. If you want happiness, give happiness. If you want a smile, then just smile!

Whatever you plant in the ground is what you will get at harvest. You don't plant carrots and expect cucumbers. You will get carrots one hundred percent of the time.

If you plant bad thoughts in your mind, then you will get bad results. Good thoughts will lead to good results. Don't keep doing the same thing over and over again and expect a different result.

Plant the fruits of success that I've talked about in this book and follow its steps and you will get success one hundred percent of the time.

They call the law of attraction a law for a reason. Like the law of gravity, it always works. Unlike the law of gravity, which can be temporarily superseded by the law of lift, nothing supersedes the law of attraction. Whatever you focus on is what you will get, whether you like it or not. If you don't like the term "law of attraction," then swap it for "law of creation." You are the creator of your life.

Roman Emperor Marcus Aurelius said, "The happiness of your life depends upon the quality of your thoughts."

If someone was to paint a picture of your life now, how would it look? If you don't think the picture would be very impressive, then repaint the picture in your mind and live that way from now on.

What would you like the inscription on your tombstone to say?

Write down what you would like it to say and then start living that way from this day on.

A long time ago, the conquistador Cortes landed on the Aztec land he would soon conquer. When his men were all onshore, he had his ships burnt and sunk. Cortes wanted there to be no way to retreat. They were going to defeat the Aztecs or die trying.

Like Joe and the mountain and Cortes and the Aztecs, from now on never retreat, never turn back to the old way of thinking, and you will be pleasantly surprised that once you start applying what I have spoken about, you won't want to go backwards.

Viktor Frankl, my hero, said to himself that if no one could prove to him with real evidence, with one hundred percent proof, that he would not survive the concentration camp, then he was going to live each day as if he would survive, and he did survive.

If no one can show you with one hundred percent certainty that you won't be a smashing success, then live every day as if you are going to be successful.

Block out anyone who tells you that you won't win. Don't let that sort of talk enter your mind.

Make sure that the soldier at the door of your mind is ever alert and ever ready to slay any negative thought that tries to take up residence in your mind. You will be victorious, you will not let anyone or anything stop you.

Imagine what your life can be from now on.

You will be free, and there are very few people in history who could say that they were truly free.

No one can control your mind unless you let them. You are a special creation and you have great power. Live each day as if it is your last and learn each day as if you will live forever. You will live in a different reality. You will be able to do things that people say are impossible for you to do. You are the creator of your destiny. Imagine what you will do from this day forward. Continue to remember your power and the power of your thoughts. You can be, do, or have anything that you want. Fortune favours the bold, so be unstoppable!